METHODS HELP HOUSEHOLDERS REDUCE EXPENDITURE

JOHN LOK

Contents

Contents

Preface

Introduction

I write this book aims to give my opinions to indicate whether what factors can influence householder resource , such as, gas, electricity energy behavior at home as well as what factors influence householder rent or house purchase choice at housing market in any countries as well as to explain why and how what factors can cause householder food and energy waste behaviors and how to influence their food and energy waste behaviors to be changed to reduce or avoid at home.

Can artifical intelligence predict houselder consumption behavior? I shall follow behavioral economic analysis theory to explain why and how these factors can influence householder electricity energy consumers to decide or choose how much electricity energy to feel that it is the most reasonable judgement of electricity energy consumption in their daily life.

The factors which can influence householder electricity energy consumers to impact their behaviors how to choose electricity energy every day. These factors can include housing quality factor, every country's regional house prices factor, wealth effects on householder final consumption factor, environmental impacts of householder activities factor, the effect of occupancy and building characteristics on energy use for space and water heating factor, householder income and electricity energy acceptable consumption factor, householder individual attitude to electricity energy efficiency and conservation factor, cooking fuel and lighting electricity energy education to the householder factor, householder individual electricity energy comfortable physical feeling factor, knowledge about electricity energy usage, energy performance and energy efficiency factor, weather impact on the householder electric energy consumption factor, the annual average temperature weather change factor, the electricity energy consumption characteristics to the country's residential sector factor and the socio-demographic and psychological influence to residential electricity energy consumption factor.

I shall indicate above all these factors to explain how and why these factors can influence householders' electricity energy useful behaviors and consumption desires to impact their electricity energy consumption to be more or less daily. My readers can analyze whether these factors can influence every householder electricity energy users to change whose electricity energy consumption attitude every day really.

The first part concerns to explain what factors influence householder energy consumption at home. The first chapter explains whether the house quality can influence the householder electricity energy consumption or useful activities to be more or less. The second chapter explains environment factor can influence householder electricity energy consumption activities. The chapter three explains whether the effect of house space occupancy and building characteristics can influence on householder electricity energy use. The chapter four explains whether it has relationship between the householder income and the electricity energy needs as well as whether how to evaluate the subsidies and social tariffs to assist lower income earners to analyze household energy consumption more accurate.

The final chapter explains what factors can influence householders how to use energy in efficient way at homes.

I write this book second part gives opinions to explain whether the country's government rent subsidies support to its householders to pay lesser rent amount assistance. It will bring what influences to impact its householders rent spending behavioral choices or decisions. The questions include such as , whether rent subsidies assistance can encourage the country's householders choose to spend more rent expenditure to rent higher quality of private properties to live, due to their government can support some sent subsidies to assist them to pay higher rents in order to reduce their rent burdens, or whether rent subsidies assistance can encourage the country's low income working age group householders choose to rent cheap rent expenditure of public houses to live, or whether it will bring the raising of shortage of public house number supplies, due to it encourages many low income working age group householders choose to rent public houses to live , or whether it encourages many high income working age group householders to choose to rent private properties to live in the country's housing market, due to they can pay lower rent amount to rent high quality of private houses to live , or whether rent subsidies assistance can bring private properties number growth or expansion, due to it is sudden that the country has many high working age group householders choose to rent private properties to live, due to rent subsidies assists them to pay less rent , or it will bring negative private properties rent raising effect, due to the country has many householder choose to rent any kinds of private properties to live to cause the challenge of the demand to private properties is sudden increased, but the supply of private properties is limited. So, it encounters the shortage of private properties shortage supply challenge, or whether the government's rent subsidies strategy can bring good or bad influences to the country's householders' living changing needs in society etc. different rent subsidies assistance questions.

This part can indicate clear explanation to let readers to understand whether how any why rent subsidies assistance will influence the country's householders' living consumption behaviors change in society.

Part three concerns to explain how and why what factors cause householder food wastage behavior as well as to explain what is really exciting about (AI) machine learning to compare government and school environment protection education to persuade humans to avoid to do food waste, food or energy waste behaviours for householders and product manufacturers.

I write third part aims to let readers to analyse whether future (AI) artificial intelligent machine can assist humans to learn how to reduce food waste or food loss to consumers' food habits or manufacturers' manufacturing processed in order to avoid the actual food or energy shortage challenges are caused from human's food or energy consumption negligent behaviours. Consequently, I hope my readers can make judgement whether future (AI) artificial intelligence can help human to reduce or avoid environmental pollution or food/ energy waste challenges to cause social cost to be raised to influence human future living quality to be poor.

Nowadays, humans do good any energy waste behaviours are serious. Instead of school education and government education both provide environment protection educational message to persuade use to change our food and energy waste behaviours of our daily incorrect or wrong life habits or life attitudes.

Does future artificial intelligent (AI) technology change to householders' eating or food wrong habits or wrong energy consumption or using behaviours and they can be influenced to avoid or reduce to do waste behaviours again at homes successfully when they are using electricity or any energy to cook any food at homes? Does future artificial intelligent (AI) technology improves or assists food manufacturers to reduce food loss or energy loss in manufacturing processes?

I shall explain that how and why future (AI) technology can be applied to these aspects to assist human to avoid food loss or food waste as well as electricity waste social challenge. The discussion issues include: artificial intelligent biological techniques for food waste solutions, waste sorting system solutions etc. (AI) waste avoid methods, how and why which can bring benefits to react to change in the waste stream and to easily create new qualities of recyclables environment protection and waste reducing benefit to human, e.g. food waste reducing welfare to human.

In third part, I shall indiate how and why what factors can impact or influence householders or any energy users to waste to consume energy to use at homes or offices or any places or any private using, e.g. driving cars. etc. energy waste using behaviours , then I shall explain why (AI) technology can impact energy users to reduce to use excessive energy behaviours more easier than education method.

The factors which can influence householder electricity energy consumers to impact their behaviors how to choose electricity energy every day. These factors can include housing quality factor, every country's regional house prices factor, wealth effects on householder final consumption factor, environmental impacts of householder activities factor, the effect of occupancy and building characteristics on energy use for space and water heating factor, householder income and electricity energy acceptable consumption factor, householder individual attitude to electricity energy efficiency and conservation factor, cooking fuel and lighting electricity energy education to the householder factor, householder individual electricity energy comfortable physical feeling factor, knowledge about electricity energy usage, energy performance and energy efficiency factor, weather impact on the householder electric energy consumption factor, the annual average temperature weather change factor, the electricity energy consumption characteristics to the country's residential sector factor and the socio-demographic and psychological influence to residential electricity energy consumption factor.
I shall indicate above all these factors to explain how and why these factors can influence householders' electricity energy useful behaviors and consumption desires to impact their electricity energy consumption to be more or less daily. My readers can analyze whether these factors can influence every householder electricity energy users to change whose electricity energy consumption attitude every day really.

Also, I shall explain whether how and why (AI) systems can help product manufacturers to manage complex business using business operations and optimize decision using (AI) machine-learning tools to assist them to efficiently use natural resources, e.g. electricity, gas and allocate them to use efficiently. When they are manufacturing any products in manufacturing processes.

Prologue

Table of contents

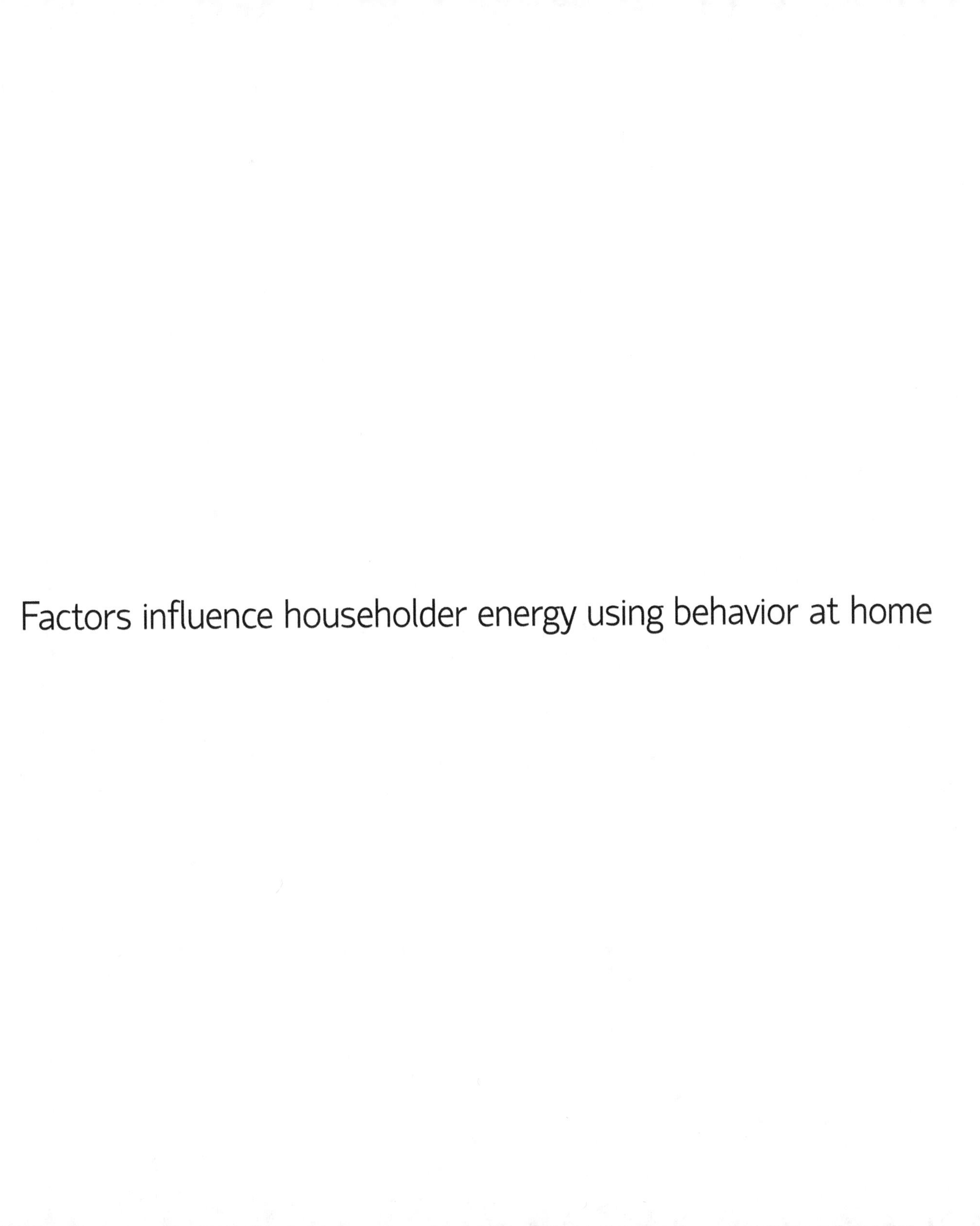

Factors influence householder energy using behavior at home

CHAPTER ONE

House quality influences householder electricity energy consumption behavior

Can apply artificial intelligence measure the house quality how influences the householder electricity energy consumption or useful activities to be more or less? In general, house owners have both intentions for whose property. One intention is living the house by householder himself or herself or householder with families themselves. Another intention is that renting to others to receive rent income (landlord). So, in the housing market, the housing consumer includes either the property owner intents to rent to others to live for rent income aim or the property buyers intents to buy the house to be house owner to live. Does these both different property purchase intentions, which will influence the householder's attitude to use electricity energy consumption desire to be more or less, due to the householder's demand to whose house quality factor influence? This is one interesting question concerns the householder electricity energy consumption desire change to the householder, due to house's investment or house's living intention influences to house quality factor.

How does house quality factor influence to householder electricity energy consumption desire to be more or less? Has it relationship between house quality and house investment or living intention to cause house quality demand to influence the householder electricity energy consumption desire change or demand to be more or less? Has it relationship between regional housing market living or rent investment intentions, housing quality and electricity energy consumption more or less desire? I suppose that the determinants of the residential electricity energy demand form space-heating and cooking, due to the property quality demand influence and the householder's living or rent investment intention influence both, which will influence the householder's electricity energy consumption or useful behavior when he/she/they is/are living in the house.

I argue that rent properties are not only consumer goods, but it also constitute financial market assets. It is therefore reasonable to assume that rational (rent income investment intention) investors choose to raise housing quality (e.g. thermal insulation technological installing at home, heating or cooling technology or artificial intelligent window, lighting, door opening or closing) in order to attract many people choose to rent whose house to live. The householder's aim is to achieve an acceptable return on investment (ROI) or raising rent income aim when he/she rents whose house to anyone, it is easy to attract many people to choose to pay higher rent his/her house to live in the property rent market. Moreover, the another important factor is that rents and future house sale prices of properties differ regionally (or even locally), and largely depend on housing market fundamentals, such as either the house living buyer's income levels or the house rent buyer's income levels, vacancy rates, and/or householder investor's expectations.

Thus, if the householder expects to rent whose house and raises rent to attract many people choose to rent whose house to live, who will attempt to install many new technology in order to satisfy their high quality of life need when they can pay higher rent to rent to choose to rent whose houses to live. Their aim only achieves to raise housing quality, but any new technology will lead to increase electricity energy consumption or use in the house.

Hence, any high quality of houses will influence the householder to use or consume more electricity energy at home. It means that the householder will choose to consume or use more electricity energy at home, if he/she or the family householder demands to live more comfortable house and he/she/they can have high quality of living life at home. This comfortable living demand to the householder (property renter or property buyer) view point can explain why the better quality of house factor will influence the electricity energy consumption desire to the householder also to be more daily.

I shall indicate one home electricity energy consumption experiment, it indicated that utilizing aggregate data on regional space-heating energy consumption form over 300,000 apartment buildings in 97 German planning regions. The study applies structural equation modelling to estimate the influence of housing market fundamentals on the level of housing quality, and subsequently on regional electricity energy consumption. Consequently, it suggests that housing market fundamental explain regional differences in the housing quality.

In particular, findings show that the level of per capita income, investor' expectations about future housing market development as well as vacancy all explain regional differences in housing quality has a significant impact on electricity energy consumption.

In the way, this experiment can indicate evidence that regional housing market fundamental have a substantial influence on regional levels of housing quality and energy consumption desires to the German regional householders. This Germany regional householder experiment found important implications for high or low housing quality of the regional property building and householders either property living or property rent intention of comfortable living feeling need factor which will influence the regional property householder electricity energy consumption desire to be raised or reduced. These factors will influence the consequence of electricity energy demand to be increased or decreased needs every day for the regional householder as well as the country's electricity energy supplier(s) can gather the regional properties whether they are high or low quality to predict the regional properties householders' electricity energy consumption supply budget more accurate. It implies that an important determinant of residential housing quality will have possible to influence electricity energy demand to be more or less for long term. IN particular, this Germany regional residential experiment can explain and find an important role in formulating assumptions about the quality factor has chance to influence the regional residential future levels of electricity energy efficiency and consumption in the country. Hence, housing developments and electricity energy firms can follow this regional residential housing quality factor to evaluate whether the regional housing market is the corresponding investment patterns as well as the energy researchers can follow the regional residential housing quality whether it is high or low housing quality factor to evaluate the more accurate models of regional electricity energy demand to any regional residential householders' houses in the country.

In consumer behavioral view point, it explains that if the country government expected many householders feel to need to spend much electricity energy or have much electricity energy useful demand or desire at home. The country government ought to encourage the country residential property or house developers choose to build many houses which have technological product installed to satisfy the regional householders' residential comfortable living need when they choose the regions to build the high quality houses to let them to live. Then, the regional householders will be influenced to consume or use much electricity energy at homes, due to they feel that they are living at high quality and comfortable and high building technological installed apartments in the country's regions. Then, the country's government and electricity energy provider(s) may be raise much electricity energy efficiency and supply and profit , due to the regional residential householders' electricity energy consumption or useful desire need is therefore influenced to be more by the regional high quality of residential houses factor. So, the regional high quality of residential house factor will have relationship to the regional electricity energy consumption and efficiency to the regional householder's houses.

Otherwise, if the country government felt electricity energy is shortage, it ought encourage the property developers build many low quality and low building technological houses to let householders to live themselves or rent to others to live in the country's different regional residential development market. Due to the low quality of properties and low technological installed to properties factor which will influence any these different regional residential householders to choose method to solve shortage of electricity energy challenge to the country.

In conclusion, to apply consumer behavioral economic theory to property development market, if property quality factor can really influence the householder's electricity energy consumption desire to be used more or less at home daily. The country's property developers can apply this factor to predict property consumer individual property buying consumption behaviors more accurate. For example, if the US property developer planned to build low quality and low technological design buildings and lesser comfortable residential houses in the region in US. Then, its residential householder target will be trended the less acceptable of electricity energy consumption property buyers to choose to buy these regional properties to live in the US region because they can only accept to spend less electricity energy to use when they are living in the houses in order to save money daily. SO, the low quality , less comfortable and low technological installed design residential houses will satisfy their living needs. Otherwise, if the US property developer planned to build high quality and high technological installed design buildings and more comfortable residential houses in the region in US. Then, its residential householder target will be trended to the more acceptable of electricity energy consumption property buyers to choose to buy these regional properties to live in the US region because they can accept to spend more electricity energy to use when they are living in the houses in order to improve their living of quality. So, they wont's consider to spend more expenditure to use electricity energy for any technological products are installed in their properties in order to satisfy their comfortable living needs at their homes every day.

Consequently, property developers can attempt to gather marketing research concerns whether how many people who accept to use more electricity energy or use less electricity energy in order to predict they ought build how many high quality or low quality houses number in different regions more accurate in themselves countries or overseas countries property development market.

Environmental impacts of householder greenhouse gas electricity energy consumption activities

Can artificial intelligence measure whether what environment factors influence householder electricity energy consumption activities? Has environment factor relationship to influence householder electricity energy consumption behaviors? Socially, householder electricity energy consumption provides us with sources of living satisfaction , but if any sudden environment factor changes, whether it will influence householder consume or use more or less electricity energy decision at home. However, I assume householder electricity energy consumption will have a considerable proportion of the environmental impacts be influenced by our way of life and our economic decision of electricity energy consumption behavior.

What different environmental factors will influence householder electricity energy consumption decision? The external environmental factors include, for example, the country's electricity firms or government changes to electricity energy regulations, electricity energy production technologies change and business practices and government policies changing etc. different external environmental factors will influence any country's electricity energy consumption to householders' consumption desire to be more or less. It will also require changes to influence the householders to consume which kinds of electric products which are needed to be used in different electricity energy natural manufacturing resources.

Why does these external environmental factors impact householders' any behaviors to influence them to concern to use more or less electricity energy power or which kinds of electricity energy products choice at homes. How any why environmental factors impact will influence householder activities at home, such as electricity energy consumption and choice? What are the key components of external environmental factors influence householders' electricity energy consumption behaviors. I shall explain as below:

Firstly, we need to know whether what external environments are which can influence why and how householders need to change their activities to choose more or less or which kinds of energy power to be provided to them to use at home. Who is householder? Householder is an individual, family, or group of individuals living together as unit in a home. Consumption of electricity energy at home may be cooking food needs, needing have colder feeling to turn on fan or air condition at home in summer or needing have warm feeling to turn on heater at home in winter, watching television programs or listening music , playing computer games or used computers activities , reading activities and applying artificial intelligent technological tools to help householders to open or close homes' windows, doors etc. different home equipment which need to use electricity energy provisions. SO, their home activities need to turn on lighting electric tools , televisions, music machines, radios etc. different equipment which need to use electricity energy provision at home. SO, the purpose of householder consumption means consumption by individuals living in a household and it includes consumption both in and outside the home. Why does environmental impacts link to householders' electricity energy consumption? I shall focus on discussing of greenhouse gases (GHGS) energy product how any why it can influenced to householders to use.

The environmental impacts will influence this kind of greenhouse gases (GHGS) energy in the product lifecycle or delivery of the service to link the householder's energy consumption at home such as these several aspects:

Extraction and greenhouse gases production (supply number), physical distribution (delivery far long or close near short distance between the greenhouse gases manufacturing factory and the greenhouse gases supplier), resources consumed by marketing and retail activities (householder's needs to use the quantity of the greenhouse gases energy product), the greenhouse gases consumers search and purchasing activities(e.g. travel to shops, internet purchasing channel, , finding the which kinds of greenhouse gases products from internet, magazines, newspapers, radio advertisements etc. different medias,) , post-use greenhouse gases energy disposal (resale, reused or rubbish). The householder's physical behavioral impact environmental factor will influence how and why he/she chooses to consume greenhouse gases energy daily , e.g. impacts of a housing development, or a wind –farm that supplies greenhouse gases with power. So, the householder's greenhouse gases energy consumption behavior which will depend upon individual personal and subjective perspectives and value.

So, the householder's useful behavior or attitude of greenhouse gases energy product which will influence how he/she/ the family use or consume greenhouse gases energy, such as the householder individual environmental protection attitude which can impact how he/she/the family spends the quantity of greenhouse gases energy every day at home, if the householder does not expect our air or water or land is polluted , due to extraction of any natural gas resources to be manufactured any kinds of greenhouse gases products. Then, this environmental pollution issue will influence some householders choose to reduce to use more quantity of greenhouse gases products every day. Another environmental factors include the bio relates the (unsustainable) use of resources to avoid wasting much greenhouse gases energy to cause greenhouse gases energy supply shortage, avoiding the cause negative impacts of quality life , e.g. noise causing when the extraction of any natural resource from lands to the householder's house is near to the natural resource extraction land and health impacts, e.g. when the greenhouse gas householder user who often use the kind of greenhouse gas product when it is used to cook or heat any equipment to cause they to breathe dirty air at home often. These impacts can be measured in different ways include: monetary costs or loss, physical quantities of resources used or waste or pollution produced and the burden the greenhouse gases energy place on environmental resources. All of these external environment factors will impact the householder individual attitude or behavior how to use or consume greenhouse gases energy product at home.

All these environmental factors concern householder greenhouse gases energy consumer individual consumption attitude is influenced by environment pollution, greenhouse resource supply shortage challenge, greenhouse gases influence the householder's negative quality of life, negative health impacts, noise, waste money , raising economic cost to the householder which will impact whether how the householder choose to use the quantity of greenhouse gases product or the kinds of greenhouse gases products or other kinds of electricity energy products.

However, these are other external environmental factors which can impact how the householder decides to use greenhouse gas product at home. They include: the changes of energy regulation, e.g. the country government has quota number implementation to prohibit to import above the limited quantities of any kinds of greenhouse gas products to any countries. So, when the greenhouse gas energy supplying quantity is decreased, but if the country has may householders who need to buy different kinds of greenhouse gases products to be used at home. Then, the different kinds of import greenhouse gases energy products prices will be raised in possible, due to demand is more than supply in the country's greenhouse gas energy product market. Consequently, if the greenhouse gas energy price us risen above the general social acceptable level to the home greenhouse gas energy product householder consumers. Finally, it will influence them to choose to buy other kinds of gas energy products to replace the greenhouse gas energy product to use at home.

Another side, if the country's greenhouse gas energy manufacturing supplier sudden changes its greenhouse gas energy production technologies to choose to concentrate on manufacturing other kinds of energy products. Then, the greenhouse gas energy supply quantities will be only decreased, even future one day , it will cause greenhouse gas supply shortage challenge to let the country's home greenhouse gas householder consumers who can not buy enough quantity of any kinds of greenhouse gas energy products to satisfy their electricity needs at home every day. Consequently, when future on day , the country greenhouse gas energy manufacturer has none any quantity of greenhouse energy products to supply to the country's greenhouse energy householders to use at home. The, they must only choose other kinds of new energy products to replace the traditional useful greenhouse gas energy products to be used at homes.

In conclusions, these non-controlled external environmental factors can impact and influence the country's every householder consumer individual attitude or consumption behavioral change to how any why the country's householders either choose to buy much or less quantity of greenhouse gas products to use at home.

The effect of house space occupancy and building characteristics on householder electricity energy use

Can artificial intelligence mesaure how much space occupancy is the suitable size as well as what the most suitable building characteristics influence each householder electricity energy useful activities or behavious? In general, society believes large space size occupancy house building characteristics factor which will influence householder use more energy at home, e.g. in summer, when the householder is living at the large space size occupancy house, who ought turn on all air conditions or fans at sleeping rooms or eating room or studying room. So, if the householder's house has two to three or more sleeping rooms. Then, he / she needs to buy more air conditions or fans in order to let all rooms' temperature to be fallen down to let he /she feel more cool comfortable feeling when the temperature is above 30 degree or more extreme hot in summer weather. Otherwise, when the temperature is low, e.g. between 0 degree to 10 degree or below 0 degree in winter weather. When the householder is living in one large space size occupancy appartment, which has thee to five sleeping rooms , even more and two studying rooms and one eating room, even more as well as every room has one heater. Then, he / she must turn on all heaters to let who to feel warm feeling when he / she is staying in the house. It brings these interesting questions.

Will large or small size space occupancy housing characteristics influence any householder often turn on heater or air condition or fan in whole house space occupancy area in order to the householder feels warmer or cooler feeling when he /she is staying in the house?

Has any space occupancy housing characteristics relationship to influence any householder to turn on heater or air condition or fan in whole house space occupancy area in order to the householder feels warmer or cooler feeling when he /she is staying in the house?

Does it bring positive relationship between turning on long time fan or air condition or heater and the house occupancy space characteristics is large or small size?

I shall attempt to give psychological evidences to explain the householder's house space occupancy area large or small size factor whether it can influence the householder choose to do long time or short time turning on heater or air condition or fan behavior in order to let he/she/the family to feel more cooler or warmer comfortable feeling when he/she/the family is staying in the house in summer or winter weather.

Does the house occupancy space size characteristics factor is the only one or important factor to influence the householder choose to turn on long or short time fan or air condition or heater in the house to let him/her/the family to feel more cooler or warmer comfortable feeling in summer or winter weather?

I feel that it is not exact right , due to the householder's house space occupancy size whether it is large or small characteristics to influence the householder choose to turn on long time or short time fan or air condition or heater time to let him /her/ the family to feel more cooler or warmer when he / she / the family is staying at home in summer or winter weather. The reason is because that the lifestyle of living quality need is different between developed countries and developing countries. The lifestyle of living quality factor will change the country's householder's expectation about the quality of living life. For example, for Africa, Korea, China , Japan, Hong Kong etc. developing countries. On the lifestyle of living quality need to these developing countries' householders aspect, that will cause a high environmental burden when they need to often turn on air conditions to satisfy more cooler feeling when they are staying at homes in summer or they need often to turn on heaters to satisfy more warmer feeling when they are staying at home in winter. Due to if their houses are large size space occupancy characteristics and they have more than at least two sleeping rooms and studying rooms and eating rooms and toilets number. Then, these householders who are developing countries' large space occupancy size characteristics houses, they won't like often turn on heaters long time to keep more warmer in their indoor whole space area in winter or they won't like often turn on air conditions or fans long time to keep more cooler in the their indoor whole space area house environment in summer .

The reason is possible because that the developing countries' householder chooses often to turn on their heaters or air conditions or fans long time in their houses when they are staying long time in their houses and their houses space occupancy sizes are very large, it will bring the electricity energy to be used more to these developing countries' householders' large space occupancy size characteristic houses. It means that the electricity fee will be also increased due to they often turn on heaters or air conditions or fans long time to keep their indoor temperature to be more cooler in summer or more warmer in winter. So, it seems that the developing countries' householders are living in the house whose space occupancy have very large size characteristics and more than two rooms house characteristics in the developing countries as above. Then, they won't often choose to turn on heaters or air conditions or fans long time to keep more cooler or warmer feeling in their house whole indoor space occupancy environment when they are often staying at home long time.

Their lifestyle of living comfortable feeling are lesser than the developed countries householders. Consequently, their lesser cooling or warming comfortable demand of living lifestyle factor will change their attitudes to use air conditions or fans or heaters turning on time in order to limit heaters or air conditions or fans turning on time to be shorter than the developed countries houeholders' heaters or air conditions or fans turning on time at homes. Due to the long time turnong on air conditions, fans , heaters at the developing countries' householders' homes, it will cause to spend much electricity energy to lead electricity fee charges to be raised to the developing countries' householders ' homes when they are often staying at homes in summer or winter weather. Hence, the house space occupancy large size characteristics ought not influence the developing countries householders choose to turn on air conditions , fans or heaters long time in order to let them to feel more cooler or warmer at homes in summer or winter weather.

So, the developing countries' house space occupancy large size characteristics householders won't be more acceptable to pay higher electricity energy fee when they are staying at homes at summer or winter weather. Due to they do not often choose to turn on heaters, air conditions or fans long time during they are staying at homes. Otherwise, the developed countries, e.g. UK, UK , France, Germany, Swiss, Singapore, Italy etc. countries. In general, these developed countries' householders' living lifestyle quality needs are higher than the developing countries. So, when the summer or winter weather is coming, if the temperature is extreme cold, e.g. below than 0 degree or it is extreme hot, e.g. higher than 30 degee.

Then these developed countries' householders will easy accept to turn on air conditions or fans or heaters long time at home in order to keep their appartment in door temperature to be more cooler in extreme hot in door environment or more warmer in extreme cold in door environment when these developed countries' householders are often staying at homes long time at night after their day time working time or schooling time. Because these developed counties' householders' quality of living lifestyle needs or demands are higher than the developing countries' householders. So, they won't consider that they will pay more electricity fee , due to they often turn on air conditions, fans or heaters long time to let them to feel more comfortable in cooler or warmer indoor large size space occupancy environment. So, it seems that the electricity energy efficiency will be raised to the developed countries' householders who are living in the house space occupancy large size characteristics and they will be possible to pay more electricity fees during they are often staying at home in extreme hot summer or extreme cold winter weather. In conclusion, due to the living lifestyle quality need (demand) is different between the developed countries' householders and the developing countries' householders. It will influence the householders' long time or short time spending time on air conditions or fans or heaters indoor space occupancy size characteristics environment in order to achieve more cooler or more warmer feeling in their houses. Consequently, the long or short time of turning on air conditions, fans, heaters for the developed or developing countries householders' activities factor will be more influential to compare the house space occupancy large or small size characteristics factor to influence their cooler or warmer feeling in their houses. SO, the house indoor environment electricity energy consumption efficiency degree to the developing or developed countries' every householder house in summer or winter to the developing or developed householders in summer or winter weather , which is more influenced by the living lifestyle qualty factor to the either developed countries or developing countries householders. Hence, any developed or developing countries' electricity suppliers need to consider the building areas of property development market buyers their living style quality demands (needs) whether their living style quality demands are higher or lesser than the other building areas of property development market, they ought not consider whether the building locations of the houses' space occupation sizes whether they are large or small sizes in order to evaluate the householders will live at the building areas of property development locations ,whose electricty energy spending efficiency more accurate.

How to help low income household earners to reduce not essential electricity energy expenditure spending at homes

Can artificial intelligence measure whether which income level influences low income household accept to use the much electricity energy at home? Has it relationship between the householder income and the electricity energy needs? How to evaluate the subsidies and social tariffs to assist lower income earners to analyze household energy consumption more accurate?

Electricity energy is essential needs for every householder at home, e.g. lighting, cooking power, healthcare, sanitation, cooler or warmer temperature indoor control at home. However, for lower income household earners, it its burden when they need often to use electricity energy to supply power to any home electricity tools to do any acticities at homes. If any these countries' lower income householder earner target can not get the reasonable subsidies to assist them to solve any electricity energy tools' electricity energy poer needs. Due to their lower income leve, it is possible that to knfluence them have enough electricity supply to help them to use to cook rice and food and vegatabe to eat, boil water to drink, turning on light tools to help them to read, watch TV, listen radio, music any entertainment or essential needs at homes at night or morning afternoon time. These lower income household earners will be easy to sick , due to they have no enough electricity supply to help them to use use electric bottles to boil water or cook food to eat. Then they only drink not boiled water or not cooked food to eat at homes in possible, due to they have no enough income to pay electricity fees every month.

Hence, how to evaluate the lower income household earners' electricity fee need (demand) level in order to provide the reasonable subsidies amount to assist every country's low income household earner to help them to pay the reasonable electricity fee which is one important issue to every country's government today. It brings this question: How to evaluate or analyze or predict every lower income household individual or family earner's every month electricity energy demand (need) more accurate?

It is one essential issue to be value to consider to every country's government. Moreover, to the estent that energy subsidies must be essential to be provided by public sources to all low income household earners or that a social tariff may be designed for improving access to energy for certain low income social earner groups. Hence, how to structure the energy subsidies between energy and income levels to be better target, such public mechanisms, and to avoid regressive subsidies unfairly. For example, India and China these both countries' income poverty and energy poverty population are the large number. So , these both countries' governments need to focuse on more aggregated effects and analyze the effects of rural electrification at the local level on the decrease in energy poverty in rural low income poverty and energy poverty householders. Therefore, every country government needs to point regressivity of the subsidy for electricity. There is room to analyze to what extent low income household earners along the income distribution demand some forms of energy, and to suggest better and fair low income targeting household earners energy subsidies supply policies.

Each government does not only consider energy issues from a social point of view, it also needs have a manner to consider a possible link between energy, hunger reduction, and food security for each country's low income household earners group. So, every government has responsibility to calculate the determinants of different sources of energy consumption at the low income houehold earner level for urban and rural both populations in order to evaluate the electricity subsidies and to test whether every low income householder earner characteristics plays a role in determining energy consumption.

In general, in the use of energy measured as that for cooking, such as LPG reduces the exposure of households to hazardous, increases the consumption of different types of foods and medicines, improves the distribution of time between household memners, enables studys with more light, reduces the use of digital computer entertainment tools at home, and moderates the use of wood as fuel, preventing deforestation. These methods are the best suggestions to help low income householder earner groups to reduce time to use electricity at homes. When they spend less time to use electricity to do any not essential activities, e.g. watching television, playing electric games from home computers, listening music. They only use electricity to turn on light read, to turn on rice cooker to cook, when they feel hungey to eat. Then, I believe that these social low income household earner groups will reduce to pay much not essential electricity energy expenditure at homes. Hence, every country government ought need to persuade low income household earners to avoid to use electricity to do any not essential activities in order to raise electricity energy consumption in long term time.

It will bring less amount of energy subsidies expenditure benefits to every country's government. Hence, the success to persuade any countries' low income household earners to reduce to spend much time to do any electric entertainment activities of consumption behaviors at homes often. This is the most efficient and the most successful energy subsidiary method to help them to reduce electricity energy expenditure when they are staying at homes. Hence, if any country government expected the low income household earners can continue really reduce electricity energy expenditure, they need to learn to do the meaning essential activities which are needed to use electricity at home habitally. Then, they can change their electricity useful entertainment living habit, e.g. using computers to play games, listening music, watching television entertainment habits at homes to cause essential daily needs of electricity useful living habit, e.f. using cookers to cook rice or cook food to eat, turning on lights to read , turning on heaters to bath, turning on air conditions to keep cool temperature or turning on heaters to keep warm temperature at homes. Consequently, they won't need to pay much electricity expenditure at home, due to their waste useful electricity entetainment living habits have changed to do any essential useful electricity activities at homes.

Another kind of method to reduce the determinants of energy demand to the low income householder earners. The governments can persuade them to consider the variation factor can influence their electricity energy expenditure are increased or decreased at homes. It is not the electricity or gas price is increased from the electricity suppliers. It is that their bad living habits of waste electricity or gas to do any not essential activities at homes. e.g. the householder often turn on light tools to read or listen music or watch television in whole night, he/she ought need to sleep at night, but he/she does not go to bed to sleep in whole night. He/she chooses to turn on light to do these activities. Then, he/she will waste much electricity at whole night. Also, some householders like to bath more than half hour, even one hour, when it is winter, they need to turn on heaters to provide electricity to cause the bath room has warm water to provide to them to bath, Their long time bathing behaviors will be also waste electricity or gas energy from long time heating in bath rooms. So, they need to change their waste electricity consumption living behaviors at homes.

So, I suggest that some low income household earners will need to be taught to change their bad using electricity enery living habits from governments' public relation promotion in order to change the low income household earners' bad or incorrected useful electricity or gas living attitude to achieve and to avoid them often to do electricity or gas energy waste behaviors at homes. So, different countries' governments need to teach them how to do the correct or right electricty or gas useful activities (living habits) or let them know or feel how to use their electricity or gas which can help them to reduce to waste the not essential extra electricity or gas energy. Consequently, they must reduce electricity or gas expenditure as well as electricity or gas shortage challenge won't be caused by their electricity or gas useful waste behaviors (activities) at homes.

In conclusion, energy subsidies method is not the best solution to help low income household earners to reduce to use electricity or gas energy. Because it is only short term benefit to reduce their electricity or gas expenditure at homes. The best solution is that to let them to know or feel why and how they have responsibilities to change their incorrent or wrong electricity or gas consumption bad habits in order to avoid global electricity or gas energy is waste to be used, even it is caused shortage from householders' energy waste behaviors.

Factors influence householder energy efficient consumption behaviors at homes

Can artificial intelligence measure how householder uses energy level at home ? What factors can influence householders how to use energy in efficient way at homes. It depends on different countries householders' living habits to cause their choices to use energy efficiently at homes. In general, global householders energy every day consumption or use aims include cooking, heating, and cooling or warming rooms, lighting , water-boiled use and computer playing games entertainment etc. activities at homes every day. Some activities are often essential at homes, e.g. cooking, cooling or warming temperature in rooms, lighting , water-boiled use. So, their activities must not avoid to use energy at homes often. Otherwise, some activities are not essential at homes, e.g. playing entertainment games from computers, cooling rooms in summer, listening music, watching television etc. these activities. The householder can choose either to use energy to turn on these equipment tools or not to do these non essential activities at homes often. In general, householders rely on energy to make ourselves lives comfortable, productive and enjoyable. However, global householders need to learn how we can use energy resources wisely because global every householder has responsibility to manage resources includes: reducing total energy use and using energy more efficiently in order to avoid energy shortage crise occurrence. The choices are make about how we use energy, e.g. turning machines off when not in use of choosing to buy energy efficieny appliances will have increasing impacts on the quality of our environment and lives.

Energy conservation includes any behavior that results in the use of less energy. Energy efficiency involves the use of technology that requires less energy to perform the same function. For example, a compact fluorescent light buld that uses less energy to produce the same amount of light as an incandescent light buib is an example of energy efficiency. So, a householder's decision to place an incanadescent light bulb with compact fluorescent is an example of energy conservation. So, as individuals, every countries' householder choices and actions can result in a significant reduction in the amount of energy used in each sector of the economy.

So, I bring this interesting question: What factors can influence householder to choose to do any efficient energy consumption or useful behaviors at homes? I believe every countries' householders will have their different living attitudes and their living attitudes can influence their behaviors or activities to choose hoe to use energy at home. I shall indicate some countries' householders' living attitudes to explain the factors can influence them to use energy efficiency at homes as below:

● Is the low income and rising price of modern fuels both factors best to influence Nigeria householders choose to use energy efficiently?

Firstly, for Nigeria householders energy consumption habit at homes example, it is richly with natural resources, modern energy resources which provide many householders with biomass (mostly firewood) and some other householders modern energy sources, such as kevosene, liquefied, petroleum, gas and electricity for their use. So, it is one country which can manufacture to provide energy for itself to use. It doesn't need to depend on other countries to import any kinds of energy to householders to buy to use at homes. But, it has social challenge, the poverty problem in Nigeria goes beyond low income, savings and growth rate, due to its low level of education, poor governamce, high level of unemployment factors influence.

It is important to know how Nigeria householders meet their basic energy needs between poverty and energy can bde described in terms of quality and quantity of energy used. Generally, most poor householders use biomass fuels because of affordability and they (householders) do not have energy equipment (such as, gas cookers, electric cookers etc.) . So, it seems Nigeria householders won't demand their living quality to be improved. It implies that they will use any kinds of energy efficiently at homes, e.g. gas, electricity, due to they find themselves in energy poverty. Although, this country has enough nature resources to manufacture energy to provide to householders to use, but due to many people are low income group, so they won't spend too much expenditure to buy much energy to use at homes. So, the rising prices of modern fuels, such as liquefied, petroleum , gas (LPG) and electricity and their erratic supply have made many householders revert to the use of traditional fuel, such as firewood and charcoal.

It brings this questions: Is the low income and rising price of modern fuels both factors best to influence Nigeria householders choose to use energy efficiently?

The hypothes is predicated on the economic theory of consumer behavior. However, when income increases, householders not only consume more of the same goods, they also need higher quality . So, it applies economic theory to householder's energy consumption behavior at home. It explains why low living standards induce greater dependence on firewood and other biomass fuels owing to a combination of income and substitution effects, such as Nigeria low income household energy home users case. it explains why Nigeria householders can accept to use firewood and charaval traditional energy to replace liquefied, petroleum , gas (LPG) and electricity modern energy . So, economic theory explains the Nigeria household energy users why they can accept to use traditional energy to replace modern energy and their energy useful or consumption behaviors are efficient at homes. Although, Nigeria has enough natural resource to manufacture modern energy to supply to householders to use at homes. But, due to these modern energy products prices are raised to the price level of householders who can not accept. it causes to Nigeria householders only choose to buy the cheap biomass, firewoods to replace high price of modern energy products to use at home often. So, they can accept their quality of living to be fallen down. So, expensive modern energy product price is one factor to influence some countries' householders to choose to buy cheap traditional poor quality of nature energy, e.g. firewood or biomass, to use at homes. Hence, they can raise energy efficiency to use when they choose to use traditional nature energy to replace modern nature energy at homes.

● Does season factor influence New Zealand householders' energy consumption behaviors at homes

Secondly, for New Zealand householders energy consumption habits at homes , for example, their living quality needs are general comfortable need feeling. Their countries' houses of space heating was found to average 34% of total housholder energy use. The relation to space heating includes low indirect temperature are associated with persistent under-heating , whether some space heating sources tend to be higher or lower in winter indoor temperature than others and winter indoor temperatures are compared to international benchmarks and established healthy temperature ranges. So, New Zealand occupant's perceptions of winter indoor temperature conditions are presented and explored in relation to heating patterns and household energy consumption. So, it seems that NZ winter temperature is low. Moreover, it will influence householders need to turn on heaters to keep more warmer feeling indoor. Then, they will use more electricity energy. In special, if the householders' houses spaces are large sizes . Hence, their heaters need long time to keep whole houses' areas or spaces or rooms temperature to be rised up in order to let they do not feel very cold in winter. So, NZ's winter extreme cold weather will influence householders' energy use or consumption to be increased in winter.

The electricity efficiency to every NZ householder is very high in winter to compare spring, summer, autumn seasons. Hence, if NZ electricity suppliers expected to forecast electricity consumption more accurate in NZ. In order to ease the life for both electric net designers and electricity suppliers, it was decided to find out, how the NZ weather conditions and every householder's house space size factors to influence the power consumption to NZ householders. If there is a clear trend observed , then this relation can be used for power consumption forecasts to NZ householders.

Why does NZ weather condition factor and householder's house space size factor can predict householders' electricity consumption at homes. Due to geographic location on the global the lowest south sets specific conditions for weather, such as NZ's south island geographic location is near to south ocean in our earth. It is a country where average annual temperatures are well between 10 degree to below 10 degree at NZ south island special geographic location to near to the sourth ocean in our earth at the same time.

However, large part of mankind is living in the conditions where there are four different seasons in NZ geographic location, dark winter, which is cold and snowy, spring with rising temperature and high precipitation, sunny , dry and rather hot summer, and windy and wet autumn. These conditions lead to different patterns in electric appliances use in NZ householders, in special, in NZ south island householders. If trends in electric energy use have substantial correlation with weather conditions, this can help NZ electric energy suppliers and producers to forecast electricity consumption and thus organize and manage production of electric energy.

Consequently, it will lead to much more stability in energy supply to NZ every householder. For example, when the NZ energy supplier gathers data concerns every householder's house space size data, e.g. the house has how many sleeping rooms, toilets, bath rooms, eating rooms and reading rooms number, even the house has how many family members are living in every NZ geographical location. Then if it can follow different location of NZ houses spaces sizes whether they are large or small space size as well as whethe every house has how many family members are living to evaluate whether how much electricity efficiency can satisfy their comfortable living needs in winter. Then, it can evaluate whether they will use how much electricity efficiency for their needs in different seasons. If in winter, many householders are living in the large space size house in the geographic location. Then, it is possible that the geographic location is householders will use much electricity efficiency and where geographic location hosueholders who will be possible to pay the most highest electricity fee to compare the other geographic location of small space size of house householders. Hence, weather factor is the most influential to change NZ householders ' electricity energy consumption behaviors at homes.

● Urbanization level and income per capita both tangible factors as well as temperature (weather variation factor) will have close relationship to influence China householder energy consumption or useful needs at home every day For China householder energy consumption habit example, what factors can determine to impact this country's householders energy useful behavior at homes? Can the impacts of these factors be quntified? What are China householder energy consumption trends and characteristics? I shall explan as below:

I believe the influential factors include these three aspects to China householder energy users: Income per capita, urbanization level an annual average temperature (weather). These factors will influence any China householder energy useful or consumption behavior at homes.

Temperature (weather variation factor) is intangible from eastern region to western region of Chin, variances largely depend upon economic level and the provincial level. So, some regions were warmer and cooler temperature will influence the regional China householder how to use electricity. In addition, th influence of urbanization level varies according to income level as well as the urbanization level has more significant impact on the structure and efficiency of China householder energy consumption thatn on its quantity. So, the urbanization level and income per capita both tangible factors will have close relationship to influence China householder energy consumption or useful needs at home every day. Moreover, these two tangible factors (urbanization level and income per capita both factors) have the more influential to impact China any one of household family energy consumption or useful habit to compare temperature factor at home. Because temperature can only influence than to choose to turn on heaters to keep more cooler in summer or turn on air conditions (fans) to keep more warmer in winter.

The electricity energy needs for these equopment tools which will be influenced less. Otherwise, the urbanization level and income per family householder how to choose to spend more or less electricity or gas etc. energy at homes. Because in behavioral economy view point, when individual householder has more income and the urban in the China geographic location is lising many high income and high household families memebrs to every house.

Then, the urbanization household energy household enery useful or consumption level will be raised. Such as China household electricity users case, e.g. large cities have many high income and many houses have more than four families members to live on one house together. Then, the electricity or gas energy efficiency will be influenced to rise. The city urbanization and per capita income level is high to these large cities have high to income population, who are living in these cities in China.

Moreover, the impact of lifestyle on energy use mainly reflects types and purposes of fuels are chosen by different China households factor which will influence the urbanization level of energy choice use. China is a country with typical binary economics and social diversity and these is significant difference in the consumption pattern between urban and rural regions. Urban residents consume high-quality energy, such as electricity, natural gas , heating power, solar energy and gasoline. For rural residents, usually use coal, and bismass energy because they are cheaper price energy products which requires much time and labor and are heavy indoor pollutants . The difference in energy consumption pattern between urban and rural China residents is closely related related to living of quality needs, building structure, e.g. steel or stone etc. different materials, manufacture, easily access clean and effective feels through the electric grid, natural gas network and district heating systems.

Therefore, it explains why urbanization level is as an integrated variable reflecting social progress situation to influence urban and rural regions, such as large cities , small cities and rural countryside regions' household energy consumption or useful behaviors which have differnet kinds of fuel useful demands and energy efficiencies qualify and quantity demand, or needs at homes. Consequently, it explains, urbanization level and income per captia level both factors are more influential to China household energy consumption at home to compare temperature (weather , seasonal) factor.

● Employment rates or gross domestic product macro economic variation factor, residential space size factor, and the government's implementation of energy labeling schemes provide significant impacts on Taiwan residential electricity consumption .

For Taiwan householder electricity consumption characteristics in the residential sector, which has different factors and pattern to compare China householder electricity householder electricity consumption habit at home. Although, they are the same Asia country. I shall explain these reasons as below:

For Taiwan electricity householder factors influence their energy useful or consumption behaviors at homes. The main factors can influence their electricity energy useful patterns include: employment rates or gross domestic product macro economic variation factor, residential space size factor, and the government's implementation of energy labeling schemes provide significant impacts on Taiwan residential electricity consumption . However, the impacts of electricity raising price and the energy supply reducing shortage efficiency standards do not significant to influence the Taiwan residential electricity consumption behavior at sources.

It means that it won't influence Taiwan householders to use electricity or gas or any kinds of energy number to be reduced, even the Taiwan government energy suppliers sudden raise, any kinds of energy price and reduce to supply energy to satisfy Taiwan householders daily essential needs at homes.

In fact, Taiwan had improved gross domestic product (GDP) and it had raised employment rates recently. So, many Taiwanese has jobs to work, due to Taiwan economy had improved to be better. So, growth had also raised. The economy improvement causes many Taiwanese had enough jobs to work, due to new businesses are set up. Many consumers excit any kinds of businesses are invested to Taiwan from overseas or local investors. So, consumption is grown, the electricity consuming applicances are selected, as the household consumer focus grousp number if also influenced to be increased. So, Taiwan economy had improved to be better, it will encourage many electricity consuming applicances products are encouraged to excited to be selected to seel in Taiwan. Due to many different kinds of electricity consuming appliances are supplied to attract Taiwanese to choose to buy to bring to their homes for cooking, boiling water, or keeping rooms to be cooler or warmer temperature confortable feeling intention in winter or summer seasons. So, these electricity consuming appliances, e.g. rice cookers, heaters, air conditions, fans, bathing gas heaters etc. different home electricity consuming appliances will be increased to supply to satisfy Taiwan householders' needs. When they decide to buy any news electricity consuming applicances to bring to homes to use.

● Environment scientists' education message how to influence Greece householders home energy consumption behaviors from primary energy to change secondary energy

Finally , I shall indicate Greece, this western which will influence this country's householders have desires to do household energy conservation patterns or conservation energy consumption behaviors or energy conservation activities at homes. I shall explain the social economic variable, such as consumers' income and family size variation factor which can influence the different Greece family household members differences towards energy conservation preferences. IN addition, the variable, such as environmental information feedback and consciousness of energy problems are characteristics of the energy saver consumer.

Why and how can environmental pollution , environmental protection, energy conservation information message can influence Greece householders to choose to do energy use consumption conservation or less energy useful behaviors at homes. It is one interesting energy efficient use behaviors , due to Greece householders are influenced by energy conservation or environmental protection message.

In fact, scientists agree overconsumption of natural resources is a major threat to oue lives in earth. Environmental problems like greenhouse effect, ozone layer depletion, and acid rain effect are not any more problems of a specific region or environmental problem. Also, economic theory is indicated that in order to gain comfort and time households are becoming excessive energy users, neglecting the environmental impact of their choices.

Environment scientists bring these environment pollution message to influence Greeks (Greece householders) to change their energy consumption behaviors at homes. The environment scientists' message indicate that we are facing global warmth and natural resource and energy shortage challenges. Due to our Earth have limited natural resource numbers to supply to us to manufacture energy, but global population has been increasing every year. Thus, it is possible that we have energy shortage crisis. Also, manufactures are spending too much energy to waste to manufacture any products, the energy will cause air or water pollution in manufacturing process or drivers are driving their vehicles to pollute air on the roads.

Hence, environment scientists' message influence Greece householders began to consider these questions concern to reduce fossil fuel energy. Why do we need to Safety in using fuel and handle gas leaks? Why do we feel town gas smell? How is electricity located at electric station far away from town area? How to solve problems caused by the use of fossil fuels? How to reduce the use of fossil fuels?

Greece householders consider to solve the problems, the best way is to reduce thir used of fossil fuel. This helps prevent fossil fuels form being used up too quickly. Also, it helps them to reduce environmental problems because fewer pollutants are given out when less fossil fuels are used. Can human help to reduce the use of fossil fuels? Fossil fuels are mainly in power station. Although they use some fossil fuels for our gas cooker and car, it won't make much difference if I use less. Fossil fuel is not used renew primary energy. Most of energy Greece householders use come from fossil fuels, for example, the electricity we use is generated in power stations by burning fossil fuels. The buses they ride use diesel oil. Therefore, they can help reduce the use of fossil fuels by saving energy in Greece daily lives.

The actions that Greece householders can take such as: setting the air-conditioner to a higher temperature, walking instead of using lift, taking a short shower instead of a bath. This reduces the use of the hot water and thus the energy needed to heat the water. Thus, many people can help a lot to reduce our use of fossil fuels to avoid fossil fuel shortage risk occurrence.

Greeks (Greece householders) had been beginning to conern that they will face energy shortage challenge if they can not adopt more energy conservation actions. Because the Greece government began to bring negative environmental pollution and energy shortage challenge message if they often waste to use any kinds of energy, e.g. electricity , gas excessive number efficiency at homes. Then, they will be possible to fac energy shortage and environmental pollution challenge to their country in future one day. So, this energy shortage and environment pollution message has bring predictive negative worries to influence many Greece householder energy home users choose to reduce to avoid the waste of any kinds of energy use at homes.

So, their reducing energy use actions that had encouraged them to cause habits to avoid to waste excess energy to do any non essential electric appliances useful or consumption activities at homes often. Moreover, the environment protection and energy conservation message has changed many Greece householder to make decision and activities to change their lifestyle to b low living quality from high living quality. So, the environment protection and energy conservation message factor has much influential to change Greece household energy users' daily energy conservation or less energy use consumption activities at homes.

Greeks feel greenhouse energy can be environmental protection enegy. A greenhouse can trap heat in the sunlight and keeps the air inside the greenhouse warm enough for plants to grow. The glass roof and walls of a greenhouse let in sunlight but prevent heat from escape, this makes the greenhouse warm inside. Similarly, some gases in the Earth's atmosphere can trap heat from the sun and keep the Earth warm. This is called the greenhouse effect. The gases energy that can trap heat from the sun are called greenhouse gases. It is future one kind of potential primary energy to reduce environmental pollution new energy products for human consuming. So, environmental protection message influence them to consume greenhouse enegy at homes.

So, environment scientists' environment pollution message had influence Greece householders concern to apply seconday energy (environment protection) to replace electricity energy to use at home. They will change energy to use at home. The scientists' messages have more influential Greece householders energy change consumption behaviors at homes. The messages are as below:

There are different forms of energy, e.g. light, heat, sound, wind, water, electrical kinetic, chemical and potential energy. Some form energy is primary energy and it can not renew to use, e.g. light, sound, wind, water, fossil fuel etc. Some form energy is secondary energy and it can renew to use in possible, e.g. nuclear, electric charge battery etc. Why does human need to concern how to manufacture secondary energy? Because it is possible that our natural resource will be consumed all, thus we will face primary energy shortage risk. If human can invent any new form of man-made secondary energy to renew to use in order to avoid primary energy shortage to supply to use to use, then human won't only depend on our Earth natural resource energy supply numbers. We can invent any new secondary energy to renew to use again either replaces primary energy or instead of primary energy limit number supply.

What is energy change? For television energy change power case. Firstly, electrical energy changes to television power to be used by television itself, then it changes to light power, next it changes to light power. How to choose fuel form to use? Due to energy can change to different form of powers to supply different form of power advantages to supply to human to use, so it is possible that we can also invent any secondary man made renew used energy to change different form powers to supply us to use, e.g. nuclear energy changes to light or sound or heat form of powers ; electrical charge batteries changes to light or sound or heat form powers to satisfy our daily life needs.

The environment scientists' energy consumption education influence Greece householders concern how to change to use secondary energy to replace primary energy at homes as below:

For primary natural resource fuel energy example, different fuel has different feature, e.g. easy to burn, safe to use, gives out a lot of energy, inexpensive, produces little air pollution, easy to transport and store. How can we use in different channels, such as heating food, hot pat, driving vehicles.

For example, although coal is not expensive to cause electricity energy for past transportation tool, e.g. traditional coal energy train or our daily home cooking, but it has negative influence to environment air pollution. Hence, we ought to follow the primary natural resource energy's feature to decide how to apply what aspects of our life needs.

For example, if the country's people hope to reduce pollution when who use any kind of energy, e.g. US , Europe energy markets. The energy entrepreneur ought concentrate on manufacturing the kind of energy which can reduce environment pollution to be the least level to supply the country people to use, e.g. electric charge battery supplies to these countries' drivers to drive their vehicles on the roads, wind energy or water energy to manufacture electricity power supply to reduce air or water pollution ; or if the country people hope to buy the inexpensive energy to use, even the energy's quality and performance is worse, e.g. China, India, Hong Kong markets. The energy entrepreneur ought concentrate on manufacturing the lowest cost and enough supply of natural resource to manufacture the kind of energy to sell cheap price to these countries to use, e.g. China, Africa can accept to use e.g. gas, coal, fuel energy to use to compare developed countries people, e.g. UK, US; or if the countries people who hope to use energy which can easy to transport and store, e.g. light coal. The energy entrepreneur can choose to concentrate on manufacturing much coal to supply to the countries people to use, e.g. China, Arica Thus, to choose to manufacture which kinds of energy supply to the countries market people to use, the energy entrepreneur how decides to manufacture which kind of energy, it depends on which kinds of fuel advantages of the countries people most concerning.

What is energy meaning? It is defined a dynamic quality, it is a fundamental entity of nature that is transferred between parts of a system in the production of physical change within the system, and it is usually regarded as the capacity for doing work, and it is usable power (such as heat or electricity) or the resources for producing such power.

Why does secondary energy own investment worth? Because the different forms of primary natural resource energy will have supply shortage crisis, such as natural resources coal, gas, solar, wind, water, geothermal, biomass(organic material) etc. However, human can attempt to explore any undiscovered Earth or Space resource to manufacture any kinds of secondary energies, e.g. nuclear energy, electric recharge battery energy to supply to electric vehicle or space robots transportation tools to use or satisfy our daily life needs in future one day. So any kind of undiscovered secondary man-made renewed used energy resources have potential commercial worth to any energy entrepreneurs, it is possible that they can replace traditional primary energy to supply to human to use for our different aspects of life needs. In the future, the secondary energy demand will increase, when primary energy supply number has decreased form natural exploration. So, it will cause the effect of any demand of secondary energy product to be raised and prices to be increased in possible. Due to global population has been growing up, considerably China and India both countries populations have been increasing rapidly. Scientists predict there are more than 1.2 billion people worldwide will lack access to electricity, and more than 2.5 billion still use wood, charcoal to cook and heat in the future when primary energy has no enough number to supply to us to use. Hence, the fact that demand is this much greater than supply to make energy a prime market for further growth.

Although, secondary energy will have much investment worth, but energy like all other investments will carry risks. The internal and external risk factors include such as: policy is always changing to prohibit which do energy trading more easily between the energy exporting and importing countries, the secondary energy manufacturer itself own abilities to invent and to manufacture any kinds of secondary energy, improved technology can quickly make an technology obsolete, geopolitical rifts can happen overnight, the country's energy consumer (user)'s preferable choice to use which either kinds of secondary energy or secondary energy. So, it seems that (man-made) renewed used secondary energy industry can provide above-average returns, but it can also bring high risk commercial investment.

Traditionally, energy supply companies will apply those methods to operate energy providing businesses. For Shell,. Exxon examples, which had own gas stations, explore and drill for gas on their own. Other companies specialize in a part of the energy market, e.g. leasing oil rigs for example, or operating a pipeline. Energy supplying companies can choose to manufacture any kinds of energy to supply, e.g. trade oil, gas, coal, uranium, electricity etc.

Any energy price and supply is demanded on the countries energy users' which kinds of energy most choice need or certain energy commodities to be chose to use popularly. For example, if US most people prefer to use secondary man-made renew used energy more than primary energy. Then, US energy manufacturers ought concentrate on manufacturing much different kinds of secondary man-made renew used energy to prepare to supply to its domestic US market in order to raise secondary energy price to sell in its country. So, the energy manufacturer's energy manufacturing choice, it is depend on which the country's people prefer to use which kinds of energy for their daily life needs.

However, scientists predict secondary energy market will have large market share, due to primary energy will have shortage to explore to supply in our earth and future energy consumers(users) prefer to choose to use more efficiency, less energy consumption, none environment pollution cause, cost effectiveness, renew to use of any kinds of energy. For example, the electricity recharge battery secondary man-made renew used energy is one kind of reducing air pollution power to push any electric battery vehicles to be driven to compare gas energy during drivers are driving their cars on the roads. They can reduce noise and air pollution and drivers can drive safely, who only need to buy one electric recharge battery to recharge in any electric recharge battery stations on streets when the electric recharge battery has no enough power to push their cars and they need to recharge their electric recharge battery drive when they had driven between one to two days. Due to primary energy, e.g. fuel , gas, the kinds of primary energies will have shortage to supply to global drivers to drive their traditional cars. Thus, the electric recharge battery or any undiscovered secondary energy will be future driving market needs. So, man-made renew used secondary energy, e.g. biofuel, hydro-electric, nuclear, will be one kind of efficient, clean, less pollution cause, cost-effective of energy to supply to our global vehicle market, even any other undiscovered new markets. Supposing they are popular to be used for electric vehicle market globally in future one day, then their prices will be decreased and constructed to average car requires up to 1,700 gallons of oil. Also supposing that making average computer requires more than ten times or weight to fossil fuels, every calories of food eaten in the US requires roughly then calories of fossil fuels. Hence, cheap energy will be one successful factor to influence future potential energy consumer (user) individual choice needs. Conversely, ion good economic times, people are more willing to travel, to buy products, and all of which success demand and low process for energy.

In the future, secondary energy will be the best choice to food production market. The modern food production system is essentially a success of changing fossil fuels into food. So, raising energy prices are almost higher food costs and even shortage for fossil fuels energy. If one day, one kind of discovered secondary man-made renew used energy can supply to any restaurants or homes to be used to cook at the cheap price, then the profit is very high for this kind of food production energy. Thus, future food production secondary energy consumption market is large and because the primary energy inputs for agriculture are higher than the energy outputs of the food. However, future secondary man-made renew used energy for food production system is only one part of whole energy consumer in food industry. The food production is related to whole food consumption market which includes: household cooking energy market, agriculture or vegetable, rice, fruit etc. foods farming machines energy market, food manufacturing factories market, food machine package market, transportation food delivery market, supermarket or fruit/food sale stores market. They must need any energy inputs to achieve the food production or food transportation or warehouse / stores electricity supply or cooking energy needs. Hence, these food suppliers relate to any whole food factory manufacturers, food retailers, food wholesalers, farmers and home/restaurant cookers, all of them must need to use energy to carry on their food producing or food cooking or food transportation activities every day in overall food industry. Thus, it seems that undiscovered any second energy demand will be increased, when the primary energy supply number is decreasing. Also, when people can accept to use secondary energy to replace primary energy to be used for any cooking, transporting food, manufacturing food, food retail stores or warehouse food delivery energy need activities. Then, the secondary energy price will be fall down to attract many food energy consumers.

Nowadays, the food industry energy may includes primary nature resource gas energy or electricity energy for house house families or restaurants cooking needs, food delivering lorry drivers driving needs usually. If future second man made renew used energy is invented successful popular to be used, e.g. hydrogen, electric recharged battery energy for electric vehicles or restaurant/home families cooking needs or food factories machine maufacturing energy needs. Then, the seconday energy will have possible to replace primary energy to be food industry energy market.

Wiley, composition services graphics indicated that global primary energy consumption had been increasing 30 billion tons from 1830 year to 510 billion tons in 2010 year as well as global population size had been increasing from 70 billion 1830 yeat to 510 billion in 2010 year. Thus, it seems that global primary energy consumption will be needed largely after 2010 year. If future global nature resource primary energy is explored full number and it had not enough energy number to supply global human to use. Then, it will being many people feel uncomfortable and inconvenient,e.g. Some countries won't have enough energy to supply transportion tools to be driven, some homes and restaurants won't have enough energy to supply to cook to eat or to provide restaurant clients to eat etc. daily activies, due to human's much activities which are needs energy supply. Thus, it seems that global primary energy comsumption will be needed largely after 2010 year.

Wiley, composition services graphics also explianed that why the primary energy consumption demand can be needed to achieve the same level to the global population size increasing in 2010 year. The graph showed these reasons why cause the same level of global population size and global primary energy consumpion demand which may include: The graph showed that after a nation is developed, its per-person energy use hegins to level off. In North Ameruca and Europe, where energy demand has remained flat, or fallen dightly, in each of the past few years. But the 1.3 billion people on those two continents are far outweighted by the 5 billion people in Asia and Africa, e.g. Chinese and Indian. who currently have more energy need to comapre average per man to North America and Europe per man, ensuring that overall energy demand will rise for years to come.

Wiley, composition services graphics also predicted that the growth in primary energy demand. China will have 4,500 million tons in 2035 year. India will have 3,000 million tons in 2035 year. Other developing Asia will have

2,000 million tons in 2035 year. Russia will have 1,500 million tons in 2035, Middle East will have 1,300 million tons in 2035, other rest of world will have 1,000 million tons in 2035. Hence, it implied that China will be the largest primary energy need country in the future.

China will be future the primary potential energy consumer market. The primary energy includes water, coal, wind, fossil oil, gas ,solar, geothermal energy, biomass (organiz material) etc. different natural resource primary energy. Otherwise, US, UK, Europe will be secondary energy potential need market. For example, electrical recharge battery energy will be raised demand to supply to any future new design electrical charge battery vehicles in US, Europe, UK markets.

Due to US, Europe, UK people concern environment protection, so they will invent many electric charge battery vehicles to consume electrical charge battery to replace polluted gas energy to avoid air pollution when the drivers are driving cars on themselve countries' roads. For example, second man-made renew used nuclear energy can be applied to rockets to pusch them to leave our earth to fly to other space far away and consuming nuclear energy will be cost efficient, and nuclear energy saving will be more when nuclear to spend long time to be used in any long time space journey. Hence, nuclear energy and electric charge battery secondary energy will be popular to be applied to vehicles and rockets energy needs in US, Europe, potential marketss, even our daily energy needs in global second energy market.

Who are your energy business's competitors (peers)? How do they compare? How have your energy business company performed cyclically? How to choose to manufacture to sell which kinds of primary or secondary energy product(s), either manufactures only primary energy product(s) or manufactures only secondary energy products or both? Which countries do you plan to sell your energy product?

Illustration by Wilsey, composition services graphiss showed that these natural resources to energy product the world's electricity percentage, such as below:

41% of coal, 5% of oil, 21% of gas, 13% of nuclear, 16% of Hydro, 3% other renewable secondary man-made energy.

Hence, coal will be future the major natural resource to produce electricity. The energy entrepreneur ought attempt to explore any coal resources, when who choose to supply electricity power to consumers for future energy consumption country markets.

Wiley, composition services also predicted that the expectation is that North America coal will supply the expectation is that North America coal will supply Asian demand, Us export terminals have a total capacity of 173 million tommes output. China will drive 16% of the nations total output. China will drive the sea-born demand for coal over for the forcessable future. Chinese energy consumption will grow more than 12 % between 1980 and 2009 years. Though, China heads global demand, India is growing faster in terms of coal imports. Much of the global coal demand will be supplied by Indonesia and Australia. Colombia, Russia, South Africa and Mongolia are also players in global export coal energy resources.

Hence, environment scientists' education messages influence Greece householders believe that secondary energy will be one kind of new energy product to replace traditional primary energy product for human energy consumption market global needs. Hence, it is right time any energy entrepreneur needs to research how to explore any undiscovered man-made renew used secondary energy products to avoid primary energy shortage crisis occurrence. Greece householders will be the highest population number to choose secondary energy to replace primary energy to use at homes. it means that environment scientists had changed Greece householders' energy consumption behaviors at homes.

In conclusion, different countries will have different factors influence how the country's householders energy consumption behavioral changes. Hence, it seems that any country's householders' energy use of consumption behaviors will be possible influenced by extermal environment factors influence. Also, every country's energy providers can attempt to find whether the country has what kinds of unique factors to influence its householders' energy consumption efficiency to increase or decrease in order to find the methods to solve the energy efficiency demand reducing challenges successfully.

Factors Influences householder influence rent behavior

Social factor influences household renting Behavioral choice

Can artificial intelligence find what social factor influences household renting behavior ? Can rent subsidies assistance social behavioral factor influence the country's householders' housing needs in society? Why and how will the impact of social information factor influence on willingness to householders to pay rent in the country? The housing rent decisions will be determined by objective factors as well as housing market renting decision will be depended by future housing consumption desire beneficial influence as well as it is relative to current housing investment and consumption. If the householder expected or predicted future housing choice to pay rent to live because he / she feels future housing price will fall down in possible.

Hence, if the country's government can provide rent subsidiaries assistance to its householders. Also is the country has many householders feel the housing price will be fall down within five years for example. Then, it will be possible encourage that many householders choose to pay rent to live within five years. So, they country government's tent subsidiaries assistance will encourage the country's renting house market to be grown up rapidly within five years. It means that the social expectancy factor will have indirect influence to impact household housing buyers or renters' housing consumption behaviors.

However, in addition, the above householder expected or predicted future housing choice social information factor influence , other social factor influences can also influence housing activity, they include such as : When conditions are favorable in terms of house price, property taxes, fiscal incentives etc. factors. These social factors will impact how many household property consumers how to make house renting or buying decisions. SO, property buyers and property sellers both will have incentives to wait for more information about the state of the housing market before deciding to buy or rent house to live. However, the property buyers and sellers have limited information about the real intentions of transacting parties, the probabilities of renting or buying property decision will have possible increase the riskiness of housing decision.

A behavioral housing model is constructed which allows that the country householders' housing decisions of owner occupies are the outcome of interactions between objective analysis and subjective behavioral factors (social factors) of the householder himself / herself decision factor.

The social factors, such as objective process of social learning or / and the more subjective influence of social pressure, which will influence the householder's renting or buying house decision when he / she feels have living need in society. For social learning expectations, the impact of uncertainty and judgements about future benefits and costs of housing. So, every householder will usually gather information from social medias to attempt to predict when the country's houses prices will be fallen down or risen up. SO, it explains why some householders who have enough money to buy houses to live, but they choose to rent houses to live in themselves countries. Because their judgements let them to feel that there is possible to reduce housing price in society, e.g. after one year. Hence, this " after one year, the houses prices reducing information or message in society will influence the country's many householders choose to rent houses in the year. Because they feel that it is possible the society's houses prices will be decreased after this year. This " after one year housing prices reducing social information or message factor" will influence the country's many householders choose to rent houses to live in this year. They expect the social houses prices to be fallen down after one year, then they will choose to buy the falling down prices of houses to live.

After aspect of social influence to the country's householders to choose either house renting or buying behaviors it normative influence , such as housing renting or buying case, when an householder's renting or buying one house decision is affected by social media perception of information as well as the householder individual's attitude and response of others. The householder individual's renting or buying one house's decision which will be influenced by the social media information influence. SO, it makes sense to judge that the crowd is thinking in the very short-term and moving housing renting or buying markets in the country.

The information that is important that other many people are prepared to pay rent to rent the houses in the country, when the householder (either renting or buying house) consumer thinks that housing market valuations of house assets are going to increase in value, even though the householder may privately think the future house sale prices are over-priced.

These external housing market valuations information may influence the householder (either renting or buying house) consumer to make decision when he/she feels that it is the right time , he/she ought choose to buy one house or rent one house to live in the country. So, at this moment, he /she will prefer to pay long-term rent expenditure to rent one house to live, due to the housing market information indicates the future housing market valuation will decrease in order to influence he/she can pay lower housing price to compare to buy one house today. So, at this moment, it is the right time that the country can implement rent subsidiaries assistance to support the low income working age group to have effort to rent low quality of houses in society.

Consequently, it explains why social housing media factor and the country's government 's rent subsidiaries assistance implement will influence when the country's householder planners who choose to buy or rent houses to live in the country. For example, if the country's government encouraged people to rent houses to live , when the country's government predicts that the country's any houses prices are raising to above the society's houses purchase burden effort in society. Then, the country's government can provide rent subsidiaries assistance to excite or encourage many low income working age group people to choose to rent houses to live. Otherwise, when the country's government predicts that the country's houses prices will decrease in future day. The country government can choose not provide rent subsidiaries assistance to attract or encourage them to rent houses in society. Then, it will encourage many people to choose to buy low price houses to live.

In conclusion, this rent subsidiaries assistance strategy can help the country's housing market to achieve the more housing supply and demand balance between house renters and house buyers both. It is beneficial to develop the property renting and property purchase market development in the country.

CHAPTER SEVEN

Can the government rent subsidiaries assistance bring housing benefit for landlords in society

Can artificial intelligence estimate how much rent subsidiaries is the most right level to attract householders to choose to rent houses in preference ? When one country provide rent subsidiaries assistance to support people to pay lesser rents in the country. Can this country housing benefit bring advantages for landlords in society? Although, in the country's society, it is possible to encourage many people to choose to rent houses in the country. It seems that the country's landlords will increase tenants number and they can earn more renting income in short term benefit. But, in long term , it will bring negative influences to landlords. I shall explain the reasons as below:

When, the country provides long term rent subsidiaries assistance to its people, e.g. five years rent subsidiaries assistance. Although, it can encourage many people (tenants) choose to pay lesser rent expenditure into accommodation in the social rented sector. However, in this five years, it means that the properties buyers number will also decrease. Even, their properties prices will be fallen down to attract new tenants to rent the property developers' houses to live.

I believe the property purchase demand won't be raised, due to the rent subsidiaries assistance benefit to this country' people in this five years period. Hence, many people will choose to rent houses to live in this country. Even, their salaries are increased. It is not easy to influence their rent choices. Hence, the properties sold number must be decreased.

In fact, this country's properties or providers must not earn more profit from properties selling in this five years. Hence, long term rent subsidiaries assistance housing benefit to the country's people, it can help the low income working age group people who can have enough money to rant the better quality houses to live to improve their housing and living qualities. But, it also influence the middle or high income working age group people . When they have effort to buy houses, the rent subsidiaries assistance implementation will influence their mind to choose to rent houses to live in this five years, because they can pay lesser rent amount form government's rent subsidiaries assistance. It will reduce the middle or high income working age group property buyers number to the landlords in society. Hence, rent subsidiaries assistance will decrease the society's house buyers number, but , it also increases the tenants number in the rent subsidiaries assistance period. It will bring negative impact to reduce the house buyers number and the property developers will reduce houses selling profit, due to the house tenants number rises to influence the choice or house buyers number decreases in the country's house renting or buying markets.

However, rent subsidiaries assistance can also bring these benefits to the country's society, such as it encourages greater mobility within the social rented sector, because the properties developers will increase the small, medium, large different sizes space apartment number to let them to choose to rent, e.g. one small or large bedroom, or two small or large bedrooms, or more than two small or large bedrooms of apartment to let the tenants to choose to occupy. So, the property market will increase many different occupying space size of bedrooms number to let the country's tenants to choose to rent to satisfy their living needs. Moreover, it can make better use of available social housing stock, when there are many houses to used to be rented intention only. It can improve work-incentives for working age group tenants in the society, due to many people choose to rent houses to live in the country, they won't need to pay long term installment payment to buy the house in long term installment period, e.g. they won't need to pay twenty to forty years , even more installment housing payment to the housing developers. Hence, the tenants will reduce finance burden when they choose to pay cheaper rents from their government's rent subsidiaries assistance long-term. It will influence the working age tenant group 's saving habit to be better any more, due to they will have more extra money to save to banks when they pay lesser rent from government's long term rent subsidiaries assistance per month. Because of the high proportion of tenants in respect of rent subsidiaries assistance housing benefit may have a sizable positive influence to encourage their saving habits on the saving behaviors or work-incentive behaviors both.

So, the rent subsidiaries assistance housing long-term fixed amount paid benefit will continue to provide support where apartment is suitable for the needs of the tenants, and it will provide an economic incentive for working age tenants to move out from smaller space size properties to their apartment is consider larger space size apartment than necessary. When rent subsidiaries assistance can support the working age tenants to rent larger space size apartment to live to bring both working and economic incentive to improve their living of quality needs.

As a result, working age rent subsidiaries assistance housing benefit in the social rented sector will face similar choices in the private houses rented sector, instead of public houses rented sector. Rent subsidiaries assistance can also encourage the working age tenants either to occupy appropriately sized accommodation , when they had paid cheaper rent in a period, then they expect to buy the accommodation to live or they pay towards another accommodation which is larger than the needs of their long-term rent accommodation choice.

Hence, if the working age tenant still chooses to live cheaper rent accommodation , the choice is to move and a lower rent is payable. This will help to provide an additional work incentive. Because the working age tenant does not choose to pay higher rent to rent large space size or more bedrooms or better quality of apartment to live, then he /

she will have more extra money to save to bank, even, the working age tenant can earn rent subsidiaries assistance housing benefit at lower income level when he / she still chooses to pay less rent amount to live poor quality and / or small space size of lesser bedrooms number houses to live.

Hence, rent subsidiaries assistance seems that it can bring work and economic incentive both benefits to the low income level of working age tenants when they still choose to pay lesser rents to live small space size or lesser bedrooms number or poor quality of houses to live in their countries. It can encourage them to hard to work to save more money at bank to prepare to have enough money to buy another new or second house to live. Moreover, rent subsidiaries assistance will bring social attribution benefit from these young working age workers (tenants) in any countries' societies.

In conclusion, rent subsidiaries assistance implement can bring benefits to the low income working age tenants, but it can also bring low housing selling profit to the country's property developers. Hence, it depends on the country's policy implement whether it is beneficial to economic growth or improving low income working age living beneficial aims. If it felt that economic growth is more important to compare low income young working age living improving benefit in the year. The, rent subsidiaries assistance implementation is not right time to implement in this year. Otherwise, if it felt that low income young working age living improving benefit is more important, then rent subsidiaries assistance policy is right time to implement in this year. Hence, every country's government need to consider when is the right time to implement rent subsidiaries assistance policy in order to keep it's country house market's renting and house buying supply and demand number more balance between the house buyers or tenants and the house developers. It is beneficial to the country's long term economic and improving of living quality development.

CHAPTER EIGHT

How to attract young age homeowners to choose to rent appartments by rent subsidiary assistance

Can artificial intelligence estimate how much rent is the most attractive level to influence you age house renters to choose rent in preferable? Can rent subdisiary assistanc attract householders to choose to rent appartments to live easily? Some country governments indicate that rates of residentil mobility tend to be lower among homeowners than renters. It is possibly reflecting the higher moving costs to owner, occupied housing, which my cause the the old house owners won't change their old houses to move to new houses to live easily, if the higher moving costs are charged to them higher costs . So, it seems that it is not easy to attract the homeowners to choose to pay rent to live when they are borrowing mortage loan to pay installment to live the houses, even the country government has rent subsidiary assistance to persuade or attract them to sell their houses to choose to py cheaper rent expenditure from rent subsidiary assistance support. When, the country has many homeowners who are not easily to move to another new appartment to choose rent payment, even the country government can provide rent subsidiary assistance to them.

So, it can explain that the country has the increase in homeownership rates, it mens the tendency for homeownership rates rise with young age, it implies that th country's unemployment rate is reducing, due to there has young population ageing group who is working in society. So, it can also explain that why the homeowners who borrowing house mortage loans (debts) to pay installment to live the houses, they won't easy to choose to change to pay rent to live. Although, they have government rent subsidiary assistance to support them to pay the lower housing market rent for long term.

It brings this question: How to attract the young working age population homeowners to choose to pay rent to live from their countries' government rent subsidiary assistance, when they are borrowing housing mortgage loan to pay installment to live their houses?

A significant proportion of the changes in aggregate homeownership rates is. However, not explained by changes in the characteristic of the population , a possible chnge in the relative attractiveness of owner-occupied housing has possible influenced to attract the young working age homeworkers to choose to borrow housing mortage loans to pay installment to buy the houses to live for long times, e.g. ten to twenty years installment time, even more than twenty years installment time. It is possible that the appartment location has many transportation tools to provide them to choose any kinds of transportation tools to go to work conveniently, or the appartment location has many shopping centers or entertainment facilities, e.g. public hospitals , public swimming pools, public libraries, cinemas, public gardens, restaurants etc. facilities to attract them to choose to live the location. So, even the country government can provide rent subsidiary assistance to support them to rent high quality of provide houses to live. This rent subsidiary assistance policy can not influence the young working age population homeowners to change their mortgage loan installment houses to move to another better quality of houses to pay lower market rent to live, even their government has rent subsidiary assistance to persuade them to live another housing location. So, the attractive old housing location and natural environment factor and low young age unemployment factor both will influence the young age homeowners (borrowing mortgage loan installment homeowners) still choose to live their old house locations. Even, their government implement rent subsidiary assistance to attract them to pay low rent market valuation to rent another higher quality of houses to live.

Hence, if the country government can provide the rent subsidiary assistance house locations which can be close to the shopping centers, transportation tools, public facilities, restaurants etc. service facilities to satisfy the working young age population homeowners (borrowing mortage loan installment homeowners). Then, it is possible to attract them to choose these renting subsidiary assistance houses to live as well as the rent subsidiary assistance houses locations can be close to the locations (places) which have more offices, factories etc. working buildings to let them to walk to work conveniently. Then, the unemploymwnt young age homeowners can also be influenced to change their present borrowing mortage loan appartments to move out to rent these houses which are close to these working places more easily. The reason is due to they need to spend less time to go to work every time for the unemployment young age homeowners, if the country government can provide the rent subsidiary assistance houses which are built to close to th working places. Then, these renting house locations are close to the working places, it can influence them to choose to rent these houses to live more easily if their present borrowing mortage loan installment of house locations are far away from any working places.

The final factor to attract working young age homeowners to move out to rent another rent subsidiary assistance appartments to live more easily. It is the rental income maximisation strategy. What is the income maximisation strategy benefits to working young age homeowners (borrowing mortage loan installment payment homeowners)? Why does this strategy can attract them to choose to rent?
This strategy benefits include as below:

The working young age homeowner is intended to be revenue self financing, when he / she is chosen to rent another new appartment by government's rent subsidiary assistance. Consequently, combination of significant additional rental income and borrowing will be required for stock investment and to finance other activity. The rental income to various sources and it can be adversely impacted by non-payment of charges. So, low market rent payments or rent subsidiary assistances are supplemented by recovered from current tenants (the working young age population), and subsidiary assistance planning can let the working young age population to pay lower market rent payment to the country's government for either (public houses) or lanlords (private houses) in arrears rent payment later. Hence, they do not need to pay the lower market rent of this rent subsidiary assistance support immediately.

They can pay lower market rent in arrear to maximize longer arrear rent payment due to the maximisation three years period. So, the working young age tenants can save income, when they pay lower market rent (rent subsidiary assistance) in whole lating arrears whole amout is up to three years rent payment strategy. When they choose to leave their borrowing mortage lown installment payment present houses and move out to choose pay cheaper rent to rent another new renting appartment to live from their country' government rent subsidiary assistance support.

Hence, this three year arrear lower rent market subsidiary assistance strategy can reduce the working young age tenants significant financial pressures, due to the impact of welfare reform measures (allowing them to pay lower market rent maximisation in arrear up to three years period later) by this rent subidiary assistance strategy. Consequently, I believe that this rent subsidiary assistance maximisation three year rent in arrear payment strategy can attract them to choose to move out to choose to rent another new appartments to live more easily.

CHAPTER NINE

Can rent subsidiary assistance influence renters behave like homeowners

Can artificial intelligence analyze rent subsidiary method can increase renters number ? If the country government implemented rent subsidiary assistance to attract its resident to pay lower rent market valuation to attract them to live. For long time, when they will live the renting appartment for one year, even more time, whether the renters will change their behaviours to feel the renting appartmentd are similar to homeowning apprtment to live in order to decide to live th renting houses long time.

In fact, rent subsidiary assistance implementation has benefits to solve the housing raising prices challenge, such as Hong Kong has many people re living in this small city. But, the housing prices are continue rising. Hong Kong property developers aim to earn more profits when they can sell many houses. Although, these property developers feel Hong Kong has many people who will need to buy houses to live. When Hong Kong has many people demand houses to live. But, the private houses are limited to build to supply to satisfy their living needs.

So, the Hong Kong property developers will raise housing sale prices or housing rent prices in order to sell or rent to them to earn more profits. As this Hong Kong housing case, if Hong Kong government can implement rent subsidiary assistance policy to let many Hong Kong resident to pay lower market rent valuation to rent any private houses or public houses to live. Then, it can possible encourage many Hong Kong people to choos to rent appartments to live in Hong Kong. The housing welfare to Hong Kong people which will cause many Hong Kong resident do not choose to buy houses to live in Hong Kong. They will be possible to choose to pay lower rent subsidiary expenditure to rent to rent either low quality of public houses (HK government owning) or high quality of private houses (private property developers owning) to live in Hong Kong in possible.

If rent subsidiary assistance can change Hong Kong resident to choose to rent houses to live, it can also bring renting housing shortage challenge in Hong Kong. Because Hong Kong resident only hope to pay long term rent to rent any appartment to live in Hong Kong. When the renter feels the appartment is old or another reasons cause the renter expects to find another new appartment to rent to live. Due to Hong Kong government can provide rent subsidiay assistance, then it is possible to encourage the Hong Kong renters only choose to rent any appartment to live in Hong Kong long time. Hence, many Hong Kong resident won't need to borrow mortage loan to pay installment to buy any houses to live, if they choose to pay long term low market rent valuation to the landlords (private house owners) or the Hong Kong government (public house owner) to live in Hong Kong.

It brings this question: Can rent subsidiary assistance change renters behave like homeowners?

I shall give evidences to explain as below:

Many countries, e.g. UK, US developed countries have restrictions expanded to majority, center central cities, where high house prices threatn the well being of not only most residents, but the nation's economy as a whole. So, all US, UK have restrictions housing sale prices limited to manage th property sellers' house sale prices to avoid householders feel burden when they choose to buy any houses or mortgage loans to pay installments to any houses in US or UK both property markets.

Why do the US, UK housing become to hard to build in these traditionally development, friendly cities, Such as New York, Washington, London big cities? The reason is because that despite supporting houses supply citywide in UK, US residents individually have an incentive to defect and block new housing proposed for their own neighborhood. So, it implies many UK, US residents do not hope to live their houses which are close or near to neighborhood.

As this reason, it explains that why many Uk, US residents do not expect to live in big cities, because big cities have built many tall appartment and every appartment is built to close or near to another or other appartment. Otherwise, US, UK country side, there are many one to three floors independent self built wood houses and private car parks at homes which are built on every independent private land as well as the distance between every independent seld build wood house which is so far awary from each others on the countryside roads. So, UK, US city side houses are very attractive to UK, US residents to choose to live. Such as this reason, it explains why it can encourage UK, US residents choose to pay long term low rent market valuation to rent these kind self built or send hand wood made houses to live in UK, US countryside if UK, UK can provide rent subsidiary assistance to support them to live long time.

When, these both US, UK countryside residents who decide to pay long term low rent market valuation to live these countriesside wood made houses. Also , when they are living one year at least in here. They will possible feel that they are UK, US the country side independent wood made houses homeowners more than renter role. So, these UK, US countryside independent renting house lands and renting private car parks and renting private wood houses which all will let them to feel that they are these renting wood houses; homeowners. So, they will not feel that they are renters in these both countries' countryside independent housesholders. Moreover, when these UK, US countryside wood house renters choose to pay rent more than ten years or twenty years low rent subsidiary assistance market valuation to rent these countryside independent wood houses to live. It is possible to influence them living behaviors are like to homeowners, and are not like to renters.

Hence it also explain why HongKong residents can pay low rent subsidiary assistance to rent low rent market valuation of either high quality of private houses or low quality of public houses to live long time. Then, their living behaviors will be influenced to do any similir homeowners' behaviors at homes, because Hong Kong long time housing renters won't feel that they are renters role to their houses, they will feel that they are homeowners to their houses in Hong Kong city.

Hence, rent subsidiary assistance policy can help any countries residents to feel that they are like homeowners more than renters when they are renting the houses to live long time. It also explains why they do not need to move out to another new house to rent or buy to live, due to the renters feel that they are the houseowners actually. So, rent subsidiary assistance policy can lead ot influence householders' minds to choose to pay long term rents to rent high of low quality of houses to live in the country. Then, it will influence the country's houses prices can not be increased more easily , because the property buyer number will be influenced to reduce in the country. Due to the country has many residents choose to rent long term houses to live in the country.

When do renters behave like homeowners? I believe that renters will feel their behaviors like homeowners when themselves country can provide rent subsidiary assistance to support them to pay lower rent market valuation to choose to rent public houses or private houses to live in long term period. For US housing prices case example, its houses prices are experienced to change dramatically. In New York and Los Angeles cities when nearly tripling in San Francisco. Driving this appreciation is an inability of new housing supply to keep up with housing rent or purchase demand, causing the price of existing units to increase. So, if US government can provide rent subsidiary assistance to let residents to pay lower rent market valuation to rent any US public housing (poor quality) or private housing (better quality) houses to live in US these cities for long term. Then, the low wage of US workers are no longer migrating to high wage cities, due to they have afford to pay lower rent market valuation rent to rent any public houses (poor quality) or private houses (high quality) houses to live in low wage cities long tim from US goverment rent subsidiary assistance support.

Consequently, US government will reduce many societal and housing problem, when many low wage workers have afford to pay rent to live either high quality of houses (private houses) or low quality of houses (public houses) in any low wage cities in US for long time. So, they do not need to forgive their jobs to migrate to high wage cities to work in order to raise their wage effort to pay high rent to rent houses in low wage cities in US more long, because they won't need to rent any houses to migrate to high wage cities to live in US. Otherwise, if US government can implement rent subsidiary assistance to share these low wage workers' rent burden to help them to rise effort to rent any public houses or private houses to live long time in low wage cities. Then , these low wage workers won't need to migrate to high wage cities to find new jobs to work. They can have enough effort to pay long time rent, even these low wage cities ' employers can only provide lower wage jobs to them to work.

Hence, rent subsidiary assistance can solve low wage workers' social competition challenge in US low wage and high wage cities' both job markets in US, because they do not need to migrate to high wage cities to find jobs to work and they need to pay higher rent to rent houses to live in high wage cities in US. Moreover, they will encounter difficulties to seek jobs in high wage cities because there are many high wage similiar skillful workers who will also need to find any kinds of similiar skillful jobs to compete to the low wage migrating workers from low wage cities. So, it will raise the competition to high wage cities workers when the low wage cities workers choose to migrate to the high wage cities to find jobs to work as well as they also need to live in high wage cities to pay higher rent when they need to live here in US.

Hence, US government can help the low wage workers to avoid to migrate to high wage cities to find jobs and live, if it can provide long term rent subsidiary assistance to support them to pay lower rent market valuation to rent either public or private houses to live in lower wage cities in US. Hence, it is one good housing welfare to US low wage residents or workers if US government can implement rent subsidiary assistance to help the lo wag workers do not ned to migrate to higher wage cities to find any jobs to work and live in US. Then, they can feel living security to live in low wage cities in US long time, when they are assisted to pay the rent subsidiary expenditure to let them to pay lower market rent valuation to live in these low wage cities in US long time. So , although, these low wage cities employers pay lower wage to compare the other higher wage cities in US. It won't influence them have no enough income to pay rent to live in these low wage cities in US. Due to US government can provide rent subsidiary assistance to reduce their rent burden to live in these low wage cities . So, the rent subsidiary assistance policy can encourage the US low wage workers to choose to pay long term rent to live any public or private houses in any one of US low wage cities long time. They will be influenced to feel that their behaviors like homeowners when they are living in any one of low wage cities long time. Although , in fact, they are payin rents to live these any one of low wage cities in US long time.

Finally, regional scientists, land economists and transportation planners have confirmed that a householder's location decision depends to a large degree , on access to opportunities sities. Subject to budget, time and otehr constraints, it is a common assumption that householders maximize their utility by locating in a desirable a home or long term renting appartments as need to necessary and desired activities. Such as work, shopping, and recreation as possible. Also, they indicate that the utility maximization is profoundly complex, dependent on far more environmental attributes than those that can be observed and quantified, for example, people often care about neighborhood qualities, public services, proximity to relatives and natural environment offer factor.

Hence, when the country government expected to implement its rent subsidary assistance policy to attract residents to choose to pay low rent market valuation to rent public houses long time successfully. They need to consider whether the location can have above any one of these services provision in order to satisfy the future public housing renters' living needs daily. The country government's rent subsidiary assistance policy whether which can attract many residents to rent houses or not. It depends on whether the location is chosen to build public or private houses where it can provide above services to satisfy future renters' living needs , if it expected many residents can choose to pay low market rent valuation to live the location long time and let these renters to feel that they are like homeowners more than renters when they are paying low market rent valuation to rent public or private houses at the location long time in order to threaten the property developers can not raise their houses prices to sell easily. So, location factor is an important factor to influence the country residents choose to pay lower market rent valuation from rent subsidiary assistance.

Consequently, rent subsidiary assistance policy can influence some countries or cities ,such as Hong Kong, US, UK, etc. their residents feel their behaviors are like to homeowners more than renters, although, in fact, they are paying rents to live. However, rent subsidiary assistance can attempt to explain that why this housing welfare policy can threaten the property developers' houses prices can have effort to be raised easily, due to this housing welfare policy will influence the housing renter number to be increased.

(Al) technology impacts food wastage behaviors

CHAPTER TEN

Why environmental factor can influence food shortage

Can artifical intelligence measure which the lowest environment pollution level influences food consumers' good wastage behavior rises ? What are objective indicators of standard of living and quality of life? Objective circumstances refer to the economic and material conditions which are important aspects of the standard of living and quality of life. In the assessment, eight different indicators were used: CPI, GDP per capita, shopping basket, household's expenditures, GFIC basket, poverty rate, income inequality and HDI. However, these indicators is one number measure. It can't measure anyone's psychological feeling, such as health, safe emotion. The challenge concerns whether environmental pollution factor, such as air pollution, water pollution can cause human's health to be poor, even goes down human's quality of life and economy loss. I shall indicate some evidences to give reasons to support my conclusion why I believe that environment pollution is a factor to cause human quality of life to be poor , even it can also cause economy will encounter loss too.

In general, measure of quality of life need include human's psychological feeling indicator. I shall indicate, Hong Kong, China countries air and water environmental pollution challenges how to influence these two countries' people quality of life to be poor, even, it will cause their economy loss. Nowadays, China and Hong Kong and India and Afria are encountering health problems arising from damage to lungs, heart and blood vessels. Hong Kong and India and Afria and China e.g. Shanghai city pollution is a significant cause of premature death from cardiopulmonary disorders. Present level of pollution cause injury to the immature developing lings of children and adolescents. This damage will lead to life-long health problems in many and a reduction in life-expectancy. Although, there is no evidence from analyses of trends in pollutants that pollution measures in recent years have reduced pollutant concentrations in a way which will benefits public health.

There are clear indicators that for some pollutants. The problem is worsening. In fact, air and water pollution is Hong Kong and China and Afria etc. developing countries' the biggest cause of social and environmental injustice. It harms not only citizens today, but because its transquenerational effects on the urborn and youngest members of the society, it will cause its will health effects well into the later years of this century, even environmental pollution challenge will cause these countries will encounter economy loss.

Human activities have created forms of air and water pollution, such as gases from fuels, uncontrolled emissons from fossil fuels and other chemical sources have long been recognized as a cause of ill health and premature death. For example, in December, 1930 year, a dense fog affected the Meuse Valley in Belgium. Beginning on December, 3 date, the fog intensified over three days and was associated with laryngeal symptoms, chest pain, coughing, and breathlessness. Some patients showed signs of pulmonary oedema. Overall 60 deaths were attributed to the episode. After a long investigation, the cause was considered to be emissions from high sulphur fuels, including suplhur dioxide and sulphuric acid.

What is the current threat to health? the migigration of air polluton following the introduction of clear air has been followed by a period of unprecedented economic development creating new forms of pollution from the combustion of fossil fuels. For example, in constrast to the relatively large tar laden particulates from burning dirty coal which caused episodes like the London city, UK. Smog , traffic pollution now genertes fine with a different size and composition and gases,such as which may cause injury to the respiratory system and the effects of other pollutants. Such as particulates and drive the formation of the secondary pollutant ozone. The effects of pollution will therefore to some extent reflect genetic, environmental lifestyle and behavioral factors to develop these distance in a population together with the existing prevalence of diseases which may be polluted.

Hence, living in polluted urban environments is associated with increased levels of biological markers of inflammation compared with residence in a clean air environment. The damage is caused by air pollution manifests itself through a variety of common and recognized health problems, such as upper complaints heart and lung disease. Because of this, we can use statistical methods as well as clinical studies to detect the signal of changes in health problems and increased health care demands in the population. However, doctors had proved air or water pollution can cause these both curdiovscular or respiratory disease indirectly. Curdiovscular disease includes formation of arterial plaques, coronary artery, heart attacks, irregular heart rhythm, loss of heart rate variability, high blood pressure, stroke etc. disease. Respiratory disease includes inflammation of nasal, throat and tracheal airways with acute, lower respiratory tract inflammation and infection causing bronchitis, reduction long growth and function in young people. So, it seems environmental pollution can influence quality of life to human as well as environmental pollution and illness and poor health problem has close relationship.

On the other side, envionmental pollution can bring health risk, over it will influence social inequalities. Some researchers had found that the evidence has been compiled for six enviomental health challenges, such as air quality, housing and residential location, unintentional injuries in children, work related health risks, waste management and climate change. It seems human need to concern air and drinking water quality, waste management and climate change how to influence our environmental pollution challenge. Although, the evidence base on social inequalities and environmental risk is fragmented and data are often available for few countries only, it indicates that inequalities are a major challenge for environmental health policies. Irrespective of development status, environmental inequalities can be found in any country for which data are available. The valid for the exposure to environmental risk factor is also unequally distributed, and this unequal distribution is often related to social characteristics, such as income, social status, employment and education, even environment risk factor can influence human's quality of life.

(i) How environmental risk factor can influence different groups

However, human need to concern how environmental risk factor can influence inequally health outcomes to different groups. Such as, the first group is social determinants affect the environmental conditions of an individual and may contribute to the fact that specific individuals or population groups more often experience loss adequate or potentially harmful environmental conditions. The second group is the affected population groups could still be more exposed through e.g. the mechanism of education and health behavior. The third group is given socially disadvantaged groups could show more severe health effects of the social disadvantage is associated. The final group is social determinants affect health (what remains unclear is the relative importance of socially determined exposure to environmental risk factors). Thus, human need to concern our behavior can lead environmental pollution to influence poor health to alive. Even, we can not neglect how to protect our natural environment to be clean issue. Due to environmental unhealth poor issue can lead our bodies to be unhealth and to be ill and we have no health to work to influence our job inefficiency and low productivity if we often need to see doctor to raise workload to my staffs often. Then, our employers will be probable to dismiss and many unhealth employee will lose jobs and unemployment ratio will raise and DP will reduce, it will influence our economic growth . Hence, we can not neglect environmental justice and environmental inequity issue, e.g. indoor air pollution and occupational or exposure to environmental tobacco smoke pollution exposure to high traffic roads or to industrial plants pollution in our society.

(ii) How Afria country environmental pollution influences

Surprisingly, most of above countries , among of them, although Africa is a green and natural environmental country, but Africa has encounted poor natural environmental quality to influence it has poor quality of life to its citizen and poor economy growth to its society both. Why does Africa encounter this natural environmental pollution challenge? Afican have now two potential sources of pollution: consumption and production . This looks reasonable to Africa, since maintenance is completely dedicated to improving the environment, when production generates pollution only as a " by product". Capital implies the possibility of a country being trappical in an economent poverty trap by both a bad environment and low longevity. Some countries (or regions) may even experience other time, both environmental degradation and decay in expectancy. The fact that, in some cases, environmental degradation doesn't imply lower longevity may be due to the fact that economic growth might , at the same time, worsen environmental quality, but generate additional resources that can help increasing (or preserving) longevity. However, these is also evidence of countries where environmental degradation is associated with a reduction in life expectancy. It seems worsen environmental quality will influence any country's economic growth and poor quality of life both. For example, McMichael et al. (2004) identify 40 countries that experienced a loss in longevity between 1990 year and

2001 year (26 between 1980 year and 2001), they also support that the resulting world divergence in terms of life expectancy might be explained by ".... (the growing) health risks consequent on large-scale environmental changes is caused by human pressur, by both bad environment and low longevity, biodiversity and sustainable energy".

(iii) How human adult consumption and environmental quality influences future environment for human survival probability of life expectancy.

I shall assure human adult consumption and environmental quality has relationship to influence the future environment (green preferences) to provide human survival probability, it depends on inherited environmental quality. Thus, human will increase or decrease in the survival probability when we need a higher or lower life expectancy. In general, we depend on these environmental conditions to live, which include quality of water, air and soils etc. and resource availability, biodiversity, forestry, fisheries etc.

It is interesting to analyze different possible strategies to escape from the environmental poverty trap as well as factors that could push some economies back to a low equilibrium characterized. To research whether environment factor has relationship to influence human quality of life. We need to give idea of explaining whether environmental care has relationship to an uncertain lifetime. However, I suppose that an environmental kind of factor can be instead of being defined in terms of GDP per capita, capital accumulation etc. economic factors. Poverty is now related to environmental quality. It should be clear, however, I focus only on one specific mechanism lying behind environmental traps. Just as under development traps may be related to a wide variety of factors, ranging from financial to technological ones, including human capital accumulation and life expectancy. So, I should use this assumption to explain why it has relatively between environmental quality and life expectancy.

This " synthetic" indicator (YCELP, 2006) indicated environmental health is defined by child morality, indoor air polluton, drinking water, adequate sanitation and urban particulates and ecosystem vitality that includes factors like air quality, water and productive natural resources, A key ingredient of our setting is that survival until the last period is probabilistic and depends on the inherited quality of the environments. This survival probability affects the weight of the future environmental quality in human's utility function to achieve interest aim. Final stage, human will have optimal choices depend on life expectancy: in particular, a higher probability to be alive in the third period boosts investment in the environment and reduces consumption. In this case, a given country may be caught in a high morality/poo environment if low income is associated with a deteriorated environment.

John and Pecchenino (1994) were the first to introduce the possibility of multiple identifying, case for a poverty cause characteristic by poor economic performance and environmental degradation, however, life expectancy is assumed to be exogenous and plays no role in their model. Such as soils deterioration are the like, are all susceptible of increasing human morality (thus reducing longevity). So, the existence of both environmental performance and longevity, with countries being concentrated around two levels of environmental quality and life expectancy respectively. The two-way causes are between the environment and longevity. If the causal relationship between environmental quality and life expectancy involves the existence of an environmental poverty, characterized by both bad environmental conditions and short life expectancy.

Human life stage will encounter generations of three periods to get utility from consumption and environmental quality. During adulthood, when all relevant decisions are taken, adult can work and allocate their income between consumption and investment in environmental maintenance: consumption involves deterioration of the future quality of the environment (through pollution and/or resource depletion) when maintenance helps to improve it. The dynamics of environmental quality may also be affected by external factors on more resourced communities. The most importance, unhealthy physical environments across the region adversely affect everyone, ever though who are likely to be most concentrated in more burdened community which also have less social power to change those environments.

Why life expectancy and the environment has close relationship to influence quality of life? Life expectancy and environmental quality dynamics are jointly determined. Human may invest in environmental quality, depending on how much , we expect to live. However, environmental conditions affects life expectancy. In particular, some countries may encounter in a low life expectancy / low environmental quality. This outcome is consistent with stylized facts relating life expectancy and environmental performance measures. Some expects to live longer, who would be willing to invest more in environmental quality, because who feel which have causal link between life expectancy and environmental quality. However, environmental quality is a very important factor affecting health and morbidity: air and water pollution, depletion of natural resources and quality of life.

(iv) Why social and physical environmental factors have close relationship to influence economic growth or food shortage causing

I shall indicate reasons to explain why social and physical environmental factors have close relationship to influence economic growth, even human health of quality of life. The social and economic burdens of poor education, lack of affordable housing and less than self sufficient income affect, not just those individuals and families who have the fewest resources. The social gradient means that not only do whose in the bottom worse health outcomes to bottom of income group and the top income group whose will have poor quality of life influence. The higher rates of disease and disability and lesser productivity among many communities means a higher public and private burden of life years, particularly life expectancy once one reaches age 65. In recent decades, research and has increasingly shown how powerfully social and economic conditions determine population health and differences in health among subgroups, much more so than medical care. It seems that environmental factor can influence human's quality of life.

Los Angeles Country Department Of public Health (2016) indicated a country health rankings model, this department explained these three health factors can cause this health outcomes. These health factors include health behaviors (30%), it includes tobacco use, diet and exercise, alcohol use, unsafe sex; clinical care (20%), it includes access to care, quality of care; social and economic factors (40%), it includes education, employment, income, family and social support, community safety; physical environmental factor (10%) , includes natural environmental quality, built environmental quality. Then these factors can cause this health outcomes, such as morality (length of life):50% and morbidity (quality of life) :50%. SO, it implies that physical environmental factor can influence human's length of life. So, on our social environmental problems result is from a complex interplay of a number of forces. An individual's health –related behaviors , particularly diet, exercise and smoking, surrounding physical environment and health care (both access and quality) all contribute significantly to how long and how well human love. However , none of these factors is as important to population health as are the social and economic environments in which human live, learn, work and play. We refer to these factors can be as the social determinants of health to influence our quality of life. How do social determinants affect our quality of life? In the late 19th and early 20th centuries, public health concentrated particularly on the physical environment. Improvements in, for example, clean water supplies, healthier housing, sanitation, workplace safety and safe food lead to sharp increases in average life expectancy . Also our quality of life needed to be concentrated on expanded access to medical care, resulting in further expansion. So, the poverty tap is now characterized by those elements, such as low levels of : (i) environmental quality, (ii) life expectancy and (iii) human capital.

In fact, environmental degradation can have a significant impact on human health. De Hollander et. al (1999) & Melse & De Hollander (2001) showed that estimates of the share of environment, related human health loss are as high 5% for high income countries, 8% for middle income countries and 13% for low income countries. Air pollution and exposure to hazardous chemicals are important causes of the related burden of disease in countries. The transport and energy sectors are major contributors to air pollution, when important sources of chemical pollution are agriculture industry and waste disposal. Opportunities for reducing environment-related health risks are considerable. The benefits of many environment policies in terms of reduced health care costs and increased productivity significant exceed the costs of implementing those policies. So, the impact of environmental risk factors on health are extremely varied and complex. For example, the effects of environmental degradation on human health can range from death caused by cancer, due to air pollution to psychological problems resulting from noise. So it implies environmental factor can influence our quality of life in our societies. However, many factors can also influence human's health of a population, including diet, sanitation, socio-economic status, literacy and lifestyle.

De Hollander et. al. (1999) & Melse and De Hollander (2001) showed that total burden of disease, with estimated environment-related share expenditure, mid-1990 year. The average income group has 15 daily/1000 capita, the middle income group has 20 daily/1000 capita, the high income group has 10 daily/1000 capita. As regards both total burden of disease and the health conditions related to environmental; degradation. The result indicates the environment –related share of the burden of disease is greatly dependent on income, with higher-environmental shares generally occurring in lower-income countries.

On the one hand, it seems the large environmental share of health problems is primarily, due to factors related to poverty, such as limited to access to proper food, housing, health care and drinking water. Environmental determinants of human health in developing or developed countries are related. On the other hand, those to the exposure to air pollutants (particularly in urban areas and chemicals in the environment than to poor living conditions. Also sources of human exposure to chemicals are many and varied. Chemicals can reach the environments, for example, through emissions from industries, anti-fouling paints on marine vessels, pesticides in agriculture, waste incineration and leakage from waste disposal sites. When emissions of chemicals from industries and other point sources of pollution have lead to poor quality of life, source of chemical exposure. Intensive agricultural production uses chemicals in pesticides and fertilizer and in feed additives and medication for livestock. Residues remain in fruit, grains, vegetables, meats and daily products, all of which can reach the consumer.

Other sources of chemicals in food include bio-accumulative chemicals in the environment, such as heavy metals and persistent organic pollutants, which can be found in fish, meat and dairy products. So, environment pollution can influence human need to eat bad or unhealthy food to cause we have poor quality of life to live, such as the high income group or middle income group or low income group of families in our societies fairly. Other human health risks that have recently received considerable attention include unsafe livestock feeding practices through which toxins reach the food chain unintentionally. Dioxins that have accidentally contaminated poultry feeds that contain diseased animal remains can cause the so-called " mad cow disease" in livestock which has been linked to a new form of disease. The effects on health from exposure to chemicals and air pollutants vary from allergies to cancer. Although, the link between exposure and disease is often not clear, Even at low exposure levels, urban are pollutants can cause, asthma, allergies, respiratory diseases and cardiovascular disease if the exposure is continuous or long term. Heavy metals have been shown to cause neurological disorders and various cancers. In addition to , physical diseases, environmental contamination can also cause psychological problems. Noise, one of the determinants of the quality of urban life can have an impact on human health, decreasing the quality of life and potentially contributing to depression.

For Ireland, UK country example, this country politicians and policy makers believe the role of environment can be used to measure quality of life, concerning on either in its own right or relative to economic and social aspects of quality of life. Agreement on what measures quality of life and how it can be measured by the role of environment, not just in Ireland, but everywhere. The conventional approach is used for policy has been to use measure of gross domestic product(GDP) or regional valued added. However, it is acknowledged that such conventional economic measures have only a partial relationship with societal wellbeing. To the extent that economic measures are related to public products and consumption, there are also pressing issues in relation to public products and the sustainability of economic growth. However, the role of environmental factor can influence resource use and human's behavioral consumption.

Aspects to quality of life other than income include the environment, freedom, health, working condition, leisure, social and family relationship. Economists don't deny that these factors do play a role in quality of life. However, environment factor can be one role to influence other factors to influence our quality of life to be good or bad effect. For example, locations which might be desirable as paces to life (in terms of income earning opportunities or other factors) were also likely to have higher costs of living, particularly with regard to house prices or health or unhealthy air/water pollution of environment situation of the place to provide human to live. Alternatively, social indicators are based on normative ideals of literacy, low rates of premature mortality or a quality environment. Other measurement of people's personal evaluation of their quality of life, much depends on personal expectations and experience.

(v) How environmental factor can influence any country's house price and food shortage causing

I shall indicate that why environmental factor will influence any country's house price. For Ireland example, citizen average incomes and higher in the east of the country, house prices are lower in the west, who are also more able to afford a property of choices. There are more opportunities to purchase houses, where people own their own houses, who are more likely to have benefits from an appreciation is its value and to consequently perceive a higher degree of health. Generally, levels of property appreciation have been higher in the east. Unfortunately, young people and the more economically active segment of the population are more likely to be faced with rising entry level house prices and the prospect of large borrowings. So, the quality of life, such as education, crime and access to healthcare and living environment are not uniformly better in the west or the east regions. Indeed, many measures of social disadvantage are at their worst in the west regions. Some indicators of environmental quality are , indeed better in the west regions, but there are others, such as drinking-water quality or recreational access that are often worse.

Comparisons can often be reduced to an urban-rural dimension rather than a regional one. Factors such as incomes, house prices, crime levels, air pollution and congestion are all likely to be higher in urban areas in Ireland city, UK country. Why environment and housing price has relationship in Ireland to influence quality of life to its citizen? If Ireland's regional development policy is successful , it will bring with it greater competition in the housing market and greater pressures on the environment in Ireland. Because the forest will be decreased to build house, the natural environment will become wood and steel and stone of housing built environment. In fact, it appears that there is a fair of amount of agreement on the relative rating of factors influencing quality of life. Ability to own one's home and security of income were needed, but respondents also placed almost equal important on clean air and drinking water, low crime were differences. The Ireland's rural respondents appeared to place a slightly greater emphasis on key natural environmental attributes, when urban residents valued absolute incomes and social or leisure activity rather more.

In this respect, the analysis identifies three components to Ireland people of quality of life, each of which was evident in all three locations. There components can be broadly described as domestic security, social/leisure and aspects of the planned environment. The first of these includes indicators, such as security of income, absolute income, house ownership and low crime. As this component includes air and drinking-water quality, it suggests that these indicators may be associated with personal health and well-being. When the planned environment component includes those attributes that affect quality of life over which the authorities have a direct influence, for instance, a clean environment, traffic and reducing vehicle numbers on the roads in busy time.

(vi) How environmental pollution can influence social welfare and cause food shortage

Environmental quality has an undefined impact on quality of life and various indicators are used to show regional variations in aspects, such as water quality . There are many measures of environmental quality , but is only for quality of life. Moreover, the measurement of societal welfare is important. Societal welfare is not simply , the sum of the parts, but varies depending on the individual in which people find themselves at any time in their life. In principle, it should be possible to apply weights to each element of societal welfare, but as preferences for each of these vary within the population. In the absence of a method with which everybody is satisfied, GNP and GDP are typically the most popular used measures for quality of life or standard of life. But, these are problems with the data itself to measure quality of life because quality of life is feeling or satisfaction of level to the country's citizen and it can not be seen by numbers or statistic method. For example, GDP ignores household production, such as the effort that goes into the rearing of children, the benefits that this provides for society and the public expenditure that is avoided. Neither are costs treated equally with the benefits. GDP counts all economical activities irrespective on pollution appears to increase. GDP even through it is a degree of double counting. Otherwise, environmental products are good to be measured to quality of life. For example, many environmental products are unpriced. Consequently, environmental products that people value, or which are critical to the sustainability of development, are abused or depleted because of their public products have good characteristics and the absence of a market price signal.

Environmental economists try to work within the economic model to measure quality of life. Rather than questioning the link between utility and consumption or choice, the preferred approach is to add an element into the utility function that represents the value of environmental products or the stock of natural capital. By one means or another , the preservation value of these environmental products is estimated in terms of willingness to pay to protect the environment or as willingness to forego other products in return. It seems the quality of people's environment can be represented by objective indicators. At another, their interpretation will vary and can be represented by subjective indicators.

Objective indicators come in two forms: (i) economic indicators and (ii) social indicators. The former depends on an ability to select the products and services that are desires, in other words, the satisfaction of preferences . The economic argument is that people select the best quality of life, who can obtain commensurate with their resources and personal desires. By comparison, social indicators are based on normative ideals on what could be considered the food life. For example, would be infant morality, literacy, crime rates and social indicators are objective measures. Both have guided, much of the research on quality of life, particularly concerning with the urban environment. Quality of life can include natural a significant influence on local quality of life, for instance, natural beauty spots used for recreation.

Whether environmental factor is the main factor to influence food consumers to waste food

Can artificial intelligence find what the main environmental factor influences food consumers food wasting behavior rising ? For environmental quality concept, it concerns with health, safety, wellbeing, residential satisfaction and the physical sustainability can be considered to result from an when live ability can be considered to represent the interaction between the physical and the social domains. As with expenditure on the environment, investment in social capital contributes to quality of life. However, the benefits will again vary amongst individuals, depending largely on the security of their individual circumstance. As with the environment, the government can certainly adopt strategies that provide for public security by taking measures to reduce crime, a measure likely to be appreciated by everybody (except criminal) , at least to one degree or another. In other necessary to enhance social interaction, namely community centers or sports facilities. Furthermore, the creation of social capital has an statement which responds to general social trends to raise Ireland citizen's quality of life.

I shall indicate Ireland to explain whether environmental factor is the main factor to influence our quality of life and economic growth as well as to cause food wastage. Is environmental quality higher in the Ireland west regions? And if so, does this compensate for lower incomes in these regions? Is it bad that rural areas are characterized by higher costs of living in areas other than housing by environmental factor? In fact, in Ireland , UK country, population increase has a direct impact on the environment by placing demands on local natural resources, particularly open space and water. It also leads to a sense of crowding that reduces the utility associated with access to the environment. How can environment factor influence economy growth in Ireland? In Ireland, agriculture has gone through a period of significant change that has been accelerated reductions in the amount of mixed cropping and traditional land management. Indeed, changes in the expectations of young farmers will ensure that further change is likely to be characterized by increases in farm size and greater specialization with implications for landscape and wildlife. These characteristics of farm holdings are more familiar in the east regions of Ireland , UK country. As with likely to extend to the west regions as the older generation of farmers retires, although this will probably be accompanied by a trend to more farming of production needs to young farmers. So, good natural environment can provide Ireland young farmers to produce more agriculture to earn income, even who can export more rice, fruits, vegetable etc. agriculture foods to overseas. Hence, Ireland GDP will be raise if it can have good natural resource environment to provide Ireland young farmers to grow foods to sell to domestic and /or foreign agricultural market. Given the rate of economic growth, and its concentration in the east of the Ireland, UK country, it would be easy to presume that the quality of the environment is higher the further away from the mid east one goes. Thus, good natural environment is an important factor to influence the farming industry development in Ireland , UK county to satisfy their needs and to raise their quality of life nowadays.

I shall indicate New Zealand and America two developed countries to explain why which are facing environmental pollution challenge to influence their citizen's quality of life and economic growth and cause food wastage nowadays. The first country is NZ, although, New Zealand is a developed and natural environmental country, but it had been envountering air pollution annouance and noise annoyance to influence it's citizen's health-related quality of life. I shall indicate why which has this relationship between of them in New Zealand. Nowadays, New zealand population growth is an increasing demand for consumer products and urbanization have lead to concerns over the lived environments in many of the world's cities, such as Auckland, wellington cities in New Zealand. However, environmental quality is an important determinant of health, such as the bad influence of traffic-related air and noise pollution on health outcomes, specially with respect to at risk groups, both in relation to long term exposure as well as acute effect, from brief exposures. For example, cholesterol levels and in relation to myocardial infaction. Nowadays, New Zealand is encountering the high degree of air pollution and noise annoyance to influence it's citizen's quality of life. Air pollutants can be detected either visually, such as witnessing smoke emanating from a vehicles's exhaust, or by smell, such as when odorants stimulate olfactory receptors. The evidence linking air pollution to adverse impacts on human health.

Many air impacts on human health. Many air pollution health studies have focused specifically on urban area, and vehicle generated pollution in particular, as road vehicles are one of the major sources of pollution across much of the world. Elemental carbon, Nox and ultrafine particles an considered to be pollutants most strongly associated with road traffic emissions. In Auckland and Wellington cities, New Zealand , it has been estimated that 71% of summer and 21% of winter concentrations of fine particulate matter is attributable to motor vehicles. Moreover, poor town planning decisions in Auckland (and in New Zealand in general) over many decedes has meant that may people live in very close proximity to busy road and motorways within " road corridors" and so are the adverse effects of road traffic, including noise and air pollution as well as experiencing on potential for degradation in their quality of life. Such as, New Zealand is highly suitable for studies investigating the impact of roads on the health of its residents.

For example, NZ, road traffic noise and aviation noist has been linked to cardiovascular disease, hypertension and ischemic heart disease. It influences NZ resident personal psychological and physical both health challenges. In fact, NZ noise increases morbidity and mortality independently of air pollution exposure, though air pollution constituted a greater burden of disease when arise exposure had a greater impac on quality of life, e.g. NZ road traffic noise and air pollution will be caused from drivers in busy time. Specially in Auckland and Wellington cities. It will influence urban and rural environmental pollution. Some retired old people who will feel annoyance when this road traffic occurs in Auckland or Wellington cities to close to their houses in transportation busy time every day.

Next developed country is America, this country's air pollution is also serious nowadays. Because traffic jam often occurs in New York, Washington, Boston etc. big cities in US. So, U.S. cities' parks and its trees have significant influence to produce fresh air to provide U.S. residents who are living in cities to breach for their body health. David J. & Gordon , M. (2016) indicated " In U.S. these urban parks are estimated to contain about 370 million trees with a structural value of approximately $300 billion." The number of park trees varies by region of the country, but which can produce significant air quality effects in and near parks, related to air temperatures, air pollution, ultraviolet indication and carbon dioxide (a dominant greenhouse gas related to global climate change). Additional open space and other vacant lands in cities, which may contain trees and other vegatation. Contribute significant additional benefits, effects of parks and open space at the city scale can vary significantly depending on the amount of parkland and amount of tree cover within the parkland.

The reasons why parks can reduce air pollution. Parks generally have lower air temperature than surrounding areas. Temperatures are usually cooler toward the center of a park than around its edges. At night, the center of a large park may be 13 degree cooler than surrounding city areas. The cooler air from parks often moves out into adjacent developed neighborhoods. This cooling of surrounding areas tends to increase with park size and percentage of the park covered by trees. So, cooler air temperature is provided by urban parks can have significant impacts on human health. During heat wave events, which can kill hundreds of people, park areas may provide city dwellers with some respite from high air temperture, particularly in the evening, during hot, sunny days tree shade can greatly increase human comfort. Because park influences on air temperature extend to developed areas outside of parks, local energy use for heating and cooling buildings is also effected. Although, the net around effect of parks on energy costs has been by reducing temperature is difficult to estimate at least in the southern United States the effect will usually be a net annual benefit. Futhermore, large park trees will reduce winds and may provide a benefit of winter heating of buildings near the park. Although, the overall economic effect of urban trees and parks on air temperature reduction is not fully billions of dollars annually at the national scale in terms of improved environmental quality and human health.

In fact, trees and vegetation in parks can help reduce air pollution both by directly removing pollutants and by reducing air temperatures and building energy use in and near parks. There tree effects can reduce pollutant emissions and formation. However, park vegetation can increase some pollutants by either directly emitting volatile orgnic compounds that can contribute to ocone and carbon monoxide formation or indirectly by the emission of air pollutants through vegetation maintenance practices, such as operation of chain and use of transportation fuels. David J. & Gordon , M. (2016) showed "Annual pollution removal and economic benefits by U.S. urbank park trees is estimated at about 75,000 tones ($500 million) or 80 pounds per acre of tree cover ($300 per acre of tree cover). Carton storage and annual removal by urban park trees and soils in the United States is estimated at about: carton storage trees: 75 million tons ($1.6 billion), carton storage (soils) : $102 million tons of carbon removal (trees): 2.4 million tons ($50 million)". Park management is recommended by U.S. environment protection department: considering that most of the effects of trees on microclimate and air quality are beneficial for park users and nearby residents; park designs that include a variety of land cover, areas of dense trees, scattered trees and lawn are likely to provide the greatest opportunities for optimum physical comfort of visitors; increase the number of healthy trees (increase pollution removal and carbon storage); sustain existing tree cover (maintains pollution removal levels) and (carbon storage); maximize use of low volatile organic compound emitting trees reduces ozove and carbon monoxide formation; sustain large, healthy trees (large trees have greatest per tree effcts on pollution and carbon removal); using long-lived trees (reduces long term pollutant emissions from removal; reducing fossil fuel in maintaining vegetation reduces pollutant ans carbon emissions)." So, if US had many green parks, then which can reduce air pollution, also it can assist many travellers who prefer to travel to US to raise GDP travelling income growth generally.

(i) Why environmental pollution and human right abuses has close relationship to influence quality of life and economic growth as well as bring food wastage ?

In fact, environment pollution and human right abuses has close relationship. It is clear that poverty situations and human rights abuses are worsened by environmental degradation. The result can influence poor human quality of life to the developing countries' people unfairly. There are these several abvious reasons: firstly, the exhaustion of natural resources leads to unemployment and emigration to cities; secondly, this affects the enjoyment and exercise of basic human rights. Environmental conditions contribute to a large extents to the spread of infections diseases. From the 4,400 million of people who live in developing countries, almost 60% lack basis health care services, a almost a third of these people have no access to safe water supply; thirdly, degradation poses new problems, such as environmental refugees. Environmental refugees suffer from significant economic, socio-cultural and political consequences. And fourthly, environmental degradation worsens existing problems suffered by developing and developed countries. David J. Nowak & Gordon M. Melsler (2016) showed" Air pollution , for example, accounts for 2.7 million to 3.0 million of deaths annually and of these 90% are from developing countries. " Hence, our societies need to concern human right law to protect unfair treatment to developing countries people. Firstly, both disciplines have deep social root, even though human rights law is more rooted within the collective consciousness, the accelerated process of environmental degradation is generating a new " environmental consciousness". Secondly, both disciplines have become internationalized . The international community has assumed the commitment to observe the realization at human rights and respect for the environment. Thirdly, both areas of law tend to universalize their object of protection. Human rights are presented as universal and the protection of the environment appears as everyone is responsibility.

Human right and environment law can raise our quality of life because the first approach is one where environmental protection is described as a possible means of fulfulling human rights standards. Here, environmental law is conceptualized as giving a protection that would help ensure the well-being of future generations as well as the survival of those who depend immediately upon natural resources for their livelihood. So, the end is fulfulling human rights, and the route is though environmental law, the second approach places the two sphere in inverted positions, it states that the legal protection of human rights is an effective means to achieving the ends of conservation and environmental protection. Therefore, the presently existing human right is as a route to environmental protection. The focus is on the connection to influence any economy: health, food supply , housing, fresh natural air supply etc. aspects of quality of life issues. Hence, human right and environment law and human quality of life and economic growth has close relationship . We can not neglect to concern how to achieve human right law to protect our nature environment existing in our societies.

What are environmental factors affect human health in important way, both positive and negative? On positive environmental factor aspect, which can sustain health, and promoting them is preventive medicine. They include : sources of nutrition (farming, oil quality, water availability, bio diversity/bio integrity, genetically modified organisms ; hurting, fishing: wildlife, fish populations; water (drinking, cooking, cleaning,sanitation); air quality; ozone layer (protection from cancers disease etc).; space for exercise and recreation, sanitation/waste recycling and disposal. On negative environmental factors aspect, which are threats to health, and controlling them is public environmental health. They include: environmental conditions favouring disease sectors (endemic and exotic sectors); invasive biota (visuses, bacteria etc.), their hosts and sectors; environmental disruptions: floods, droughts, storms, fires earthquakes, volcanoes; air quality: pollution landing to respiratory disease or cancers; water quality: biotic and abiotic contaminants ; integrity of water transport and intrastructure; monitoring and management of municipal, agricutural, industrial outflows to the environment (gases, liquids, solid waste), human changes of the environment that: create conditions that favour disease; disturb and release noxious levels of previously bound chemicals (e.g. mercury released becomes poison) or bioto (e.g. methane released from thawed peat contributes to climate changes, create temporary, intense, life threatening heat islands (e.g. urban heat waves exacerbated by climate change); result from nuclear; biological or chemical welfare or terrorism, disruption cased by other war and violense.

(ii) What is space and environmental technology to avoid food wastage?

For example, Cananda is a developed country and it begins to concern environmental pollution challenge to announced $3 million to support the initiative strengthening health and environment linkages: from knowledge to action. The initiative will bring together scientific, technical and socio-economic information on environment and health linkages, and transfer that knowledge to inform decision-making at the local, regional and national levels. Also, Canada is principally concerned with the health of Canadians. This involves health factors in Canada and in biologically shared health regions (shared geography or exposure through trade and travel). Supports international health initiatives, such as determining health risks throught environmental analysis of disease vectors in Africa or Asia.

How can the space and environmental factors affecting health? Environmental information and environmental management contribution to the maintenance and restoration of health. Space based environmental management factors and communications can play roles in: Environmental information is for optimising use of health resources; distribution of and access to health advice and treatment (i.e. to health staff treatment facilities; short range environmental prediction for avoidance of high risk, situations and to guide immediate health system responses. Managing acute risks, adopting to them (e.g. temporary moving of vulnerable elderly monitored; modeling of health impact of environmental parameters; prediction of long term health resource needs and environmental planning and mitigation and adaptation to global changes. Large benefits are possible from attention to environmental factors, e.g. asthma prevention, disease and epidemiology. Benefits need to be quantified. This is of particular interest and relevance to pandemics , such as malasia in underdeveloped countries, potentially saving thousands of lives.

What is space and environmental technology? It can contribute to and keep abreast of environmental health forecasts (using existing models and known parameters); prepare and deliver prospectuses for what space can do in anticipation or response; steer space programs according to real risks and real accumulative health benefits, as long technical investment, don't focus primarily on threats that may have high emotional impact , but are of low actual risk; position space technology and the canadian space program in people's winds, aggressively and realistically, as a first line contributor to foresight and preduction, long term maintenance of well-being and prevention of factors of ill-health ; ongoing delivery of health services and management of current health factors and potentially capable and ready to respond in health emergencies. Finally, making the full business case for investment in space technology and space program contributions relative to the full and public and private cost of health programs. This connects not only to GDP raising, but to indicators of quality of life to any countries.

Reference

Cornelia, B.F. (1999) Rural development news, the North Central Regional Center For Rural Development vol. no 24 , IOWA.

David J. Nowak & Gordon M. Melsler (2016) " Air quality effects of urban trees and parks." National recreation and park association, USA.

De Hollander, A. E. M., J.M. Melse, Elebret & P. G.N. Kramers (1999), " An Aggregate public health indicator to represent the impact of multiple environmental exposures" Epidemiology: 606-617.

Felce, D. and Perry, J. (1995). Quality of life: A contribution to its definition and measurement, vol. 16, no.1 pp: 51-74.

Los Angeles Country Department Of public Health (2016), Country Health Ranking Model, Retrieved From www.countryhealthrankgings.org/our-approach. USA.

Melse, J.M. & A.E. M. De Hollander (2001). " Human Health And The Environment", background document for the OECD Environmental Outlook, OECD, Paris.

McGregor, S.L. T., & Goldsmith, E.B. (1998). Expanding our understanding of quality of life, standard of living and well-being. Journal of family and consumer science, 90(2), 2-6, 22.

McMichael, A.J. M. Mckee, J. Shkolnikov and T. Valkanen (2004), " Morality trends and setbacks, global convergence or divergence?", Lancet 363, 1155-1159.

Yale Center For Environmental Law And Policy (2006). Environmental Performance Index. Data available on-line at http://epi.yale.edu

The failure of human education method influences consumers to change food and energy waste behaviours

Can artificial intelligence analyze human education method is the main factor to influence consumers to change food and energy waste behaviors ? I shall indicate the reasons to explain why human education method can not persuade to change consumers and manufacturers to do food and energy waste or loss behaviour easily.

The first reason is that , food waste is a serious ethical, environmental and economic problem of excessive consumerism. Usually, food waste occurs in all phases of the food supply chain, starting with producers and ending with consumers. There are several factors which contribute to excessive qualities of wasted foods. Some are related to current quantities of wasted foods . Some are related to current production systems and product commercialization, including food quality and security norms, others are more personal like people's food habits, awareness, values and consumer attitude in regards to consumption and food waste.

So, changing consumers and manufacturers whose wrong food consumption and excessive quantities of wasted food behaviours. It is difficult to avoid from only education method , because human's eating habits or food habits are very difficult to change to reduce to do food waste behaviours in their eating processes easily. Education is only teaching how to avoid food waste knowledge promotion or persuasive method. It can not provide useful food waste methods to assist food manufacturers how to present to avoid excessive food quantities waste in food manufacturing processes , e.g. efficient operative production as well as it can not assist consumers to understand how and why the reasons for food waste, why to do the right food consumption behaviours, eating attitudes, the most reason level of consumer knowledge and opinions with respect to food waste as well as perception about the quantities of wasted food in the consumer's household. Otherwise, future (AI) technology can assist food manufacturers how to avoid and to cause food losses in food manufacturing process as well as it can assist food consumers understand they ought how to do to change wrong food habits to right food habits in order to do the right daily eating behaviours daily more influentially.

The second reason is that, in order to reduce consumer individual food waste in developed countries, there is a need to understand the factors which shape consumer behaviours. Future (AI) technology can be used to research and analysis of customer behaviours, knowledge and attitudes of people including analysis of different developed countries' consumer behaviours for food. The objective of (AI) technology research is to determine food waste attributes, daily food routines, shopping routines, planning as a predictor of food waste and policies varied in terms of household characteristics in each country.

The (AI) data gathering results can give qualitative information about food waste including data on frequency of wasting food and reasons for wasting it, which can be based on each country's consumers' food habits or eating behaviours analysis. The (AI) gathering data concerns consumers play a crucial role to combat food waste via their own households. It is important to find solutions that are relevant to food habits more easily.

Hence, (AI) technology can gather data to understand food waste problem to household level by picturing main causes affecting food waste giving deeper insight into consume behaviour throughout the every time of right food purchasing number, storage, preparation, consumption toll disposals. So, future (AI) technology (big data gathering tool) can analyse origins and quantities of food waste quantifying the scale of the problem, including all causes and food waste influence as well as to understand the variety of factors which can cause influence food waste behaviours more accurately.

The third reason is that, future (AI) technology can also be applied to solve food loss challenge. Food loss is considered to be food that gets spilled before it reaches its final product or retail chains, which occurs at production, post-harvest, and at the food manufacturing or transportation processing stages. It is also caused by poor infrastructure , and logistics, lack of technology , inefficient skills, knowledge and management capacity , it may be accidental or intentional , ultimately leads to less food available. So, it seems that education method is difficult to avoid food losses for food manufacturers. However, future (AI) technology can be applied to assist farming agriculture to grow crops to avoid food loss easily in good climate or food growing environment.

Instead of (AI) technology can be applied to avoid humans do food waste or food loss behaviours easily. It can also be applied to avoid energy waste aspect. I shall explain why (AI) technology can change or influence householders and manufacturers' energy using or consumption behaviours to save more electricity, gas energy at homes, offices or plants or shopping centres etc. working or entertainment places more easily or effectively to compare energy waste educational or learning method. I shall indicate the reasons as below:

(AI) technology is the more quality training data to a (AI) data gathering energy sector, which has access to the better , the (AI) can be integrated into its everyday operations. The energy sector is one of those industries with a wealth of data that is for machine learning and its comparison technologies to assist humans to avoid to do energy waste behaviours.

The commercial opportunities from using (AI) in this energy industry come from the technology's real-time optimisation, predictive analysis and forecasting power. For example, a number of New Zealand energy distribution companies are working with postgraduate students in big data and machine learning to analyse information gathered from both their networks and smart meters. Between 75 and 85 per cent of data in this sector is structured and machine learning can be used to analyse it, platforms using unsupervised learning techniques are well-suited for energy detections which can boost the efficiency of utility operations to reduce optimising energy cost. Machine learning algorithms are being used to understand vast amounts of data to predict mining, drilling and power generation failures and then to recommend tailored maintenance based on the potential issues.

SO, (AI) systems can monitor the emission of nitrogen oxides from gas turbines and vary the distribution of fuel to maintain the required levels of energy generation. Scaled across the network, this is a genuine opportunity to better control energy useful cost to avoid energy waste. Moreover, machine learning can also manage energy to use within complex systems. For example, Goggle's deep mind (AI) achieved a 40 per cent reduction in energy used to cool the company's data centres, even after human engineers had supported optimised the facility's energy use. ON a bigger scale, machine learning can be employed to manage the use of resources, such as water energy in " smart cities" to avoid to cause water natural energy power is excessive waste.

On benefits to energy end-users, based on real-time usage data, machine learning algorithms and supervised learning can improve energy management , even in power plants. This in turn optimises total pricing for energy consumers and provides opportunities to offer promotions based on energy customer demographics. SO, machine learning is used in some of these products as part of a deeper effort to provide customers with more choices about how to produce, consume and store energy and encourage them to do in many energy saving right behaviours.

(AI) has the ability to transform resources distribution and compensate for drastic fluctuations in energy demand. The technology will also go beyond just pricing and distribution to respond directly to the dynamic needs for energy, water power and natural drinking water and waste management. Through an ecosystem of " smart city", water and electricity can be distributed from many small energy producers and be personalised to specific regions and time frames. Each energy producers could use techniques which are particularly suited to time series data . This network would take in and learn energy user behaviours and use the information to manage the energy or water power or drinking water supply . A energy producer can then sell excess energy capacity back to the grid, maximising efficiency and reducing energy wastage to energy consumers.

SO, in the future, the key (AI) technologies in energy sector, they will bring high impact on machine learning, natural language programming, chat bots which will be applied to machine learning technology in energy saving sector to avoid energy wastage when energy consumers use energy daily. With the high volume of data available, global energy businesses can readily continue develop their (AI) technologies. Better resource allocation, improved customer satisfaction are obvious benefits as well as the most important influence is that (AI) energy saving consumption or using technology can impact energy end –users to avoid to waste too much excessive energy when they are using energy at homes or any public places or private factories or offices manufacturing places for every day necessities. So, it can explain why (AI) technology can impact energy end-users energy saving and using behaviours to be improved.

Next, two chapter, I shall explain how (AI) technology big data gathering tool how it can help energy end-users and food consumers how to impact to avoid to do wastage behaviours more influentially every day.

CHAPTER THIRTEEN

How (AI) technology impacts food consumers and food manufacturers food eating habits or attitudes to avoid wastage

Can artificial intelligence impact food consumers' eating habits to be influenced to change ? Future (AI) technology (big data gathering tool) can be used to gather data concerns to supervise or manage or control these below food consumers and food manufacturers' food waste or food loss behaviours in order to find the main reasons to cause their food waste or loss wastage behaviours in order to achieve to prevent or avoid their wastage behaviours occurrence again more easily. I shall explain to these aspects as below, they include :

On (AI) auto-supervised food consumer individual food waste behavioural aspect:

Firstly, for the original food wastage supervised, the original food which included food in unopened packages behaviours, which was thrown away because it passed the expiration date including products to like cheese, yogurts and other daily products, loose fruits and vegetables which became rotten and was never used. (AI) technology can follow these waste food gather number from different countries' supermarkets, food stores to gather waste food number in order to carry statistic analysis to find the reasons why these kinds of original food, cheese, yogurts, fruit and vegetable wastage number has increase to every month in order to attempt to find the reasons to cause wastage food behaviours , it is either caused by either food manufacturers' food losses (good manufacturing process negligent factor) cause or food consumers' food eating habits cause in order to find the solution methods to change their wrong food loss or waste influential behaviours to the food manufacturers as well as the wrong food habits or attitudes to the food household consumers more easily and accurately.

Secondly, for another kind of wastage food is partly used food supervised, the food which could have been opened or started, but was never finished. (AI) data gathering tool can attempt to follow different countries' food rubbish to gather the number data to find how much rubbish number is belonged to the country's wastage food is partly used food or the food which could have been opened or started, but was never finished to find the main reasons (factors) why they caused those kind of food wastage number is increased from food consumers; eating habits or what the reasons (factors) caused their number is decreased the country's food consumers' eating habits in order to find the most effective or accurate methods to solve this kind of food wastage behaviours from the country's food consumers.

Thirdly, for the another kind of food wastage is leftover supervised, which consist of food left or the plates or were cooked in big amounts which ended is not being eaten. (AI) technology big data gathering tool can gather global these kind of food waste number concerns every householder's food left on plates or were cooked in big amounts to every country, but not being eaten number from their rubbish.

TO attempt to find what factors(reasons) influence their food habits to do food left on the plates or were cooked in big amounts , which are nor being eaten food habits. SO, it can follow this kind of global food wastage increasing or decreasing number every month statist data to attempt find what factors influence this kind of food wastage to household food consumers to be either decreased or what factors influence this kind of food wastage number to be increased to conclude the more accurate food behavioural wastage judgement for this kind of food wastage habits to every country household food consumers, e.g. life habitual factor, food price factor, food perishable factor, climate influence factor etc. different kinds of external factors to cause every country's household food wastage behaviours.

Finally, the final kind of food wastage is that preparation residues, (vegetable peels, egg shells) supervised, this kind of food wastage could potentially be still used and not known away by global every householder food consumers, they can not be avoided to waste before cooling, due to the householder feels these foods are not fresh to eat. So, the householder chooses not to cook it to eat.

However, (AI) technology can gather data concerns different countries' householder fresh food purchasing habits ,e.g. per week or per twice week or per day fresh food purchasing frequently and fresh food purchasing number, such as vegetable peels etc. fresh food wastage rubbish number in order to find what the main factors (reasons) is (are) to cause the next month fresh food wastage number to be increased or decreased to every country householders in order to conclude the more accurate or reasonable wrong fresh food wastage habitual behaviours to cause different countries' fresh food householders' fresh food wastage behaviours habitually.

In conclusion, basing on above evidences, I can explain why future (AI) technological big data gathering tool can be applied to find solutions to avoid that food consumers to do food wastage behaviours habitually. It also explain why food wastage education method is only knowledge concept to educate to let public to know. In fact, food consumers can choose either do or not do to avoid food wastage in their eating habits daily. Otherwise, (AI) big data fathering tool can be applied to attempt to gather global householders (food consumers) their daily eating habitual data in order to achieve the more accurate and predictive householders (food consumers) their eating habits or eating behaviours analysis and concludes the most efficient and effective solutions to avoid global food wastage number to be raised to every country household food consumers. So, (AI) technology can impact global householders (food consumers) eating or food habits to be improved more better to compare education method.

On (AI) auto-supervised food manufacturer individual food loss behavioural aspect:

How (AI) technology changes food manufacturers cause food loss in their food manufacturing processes, I shall indicate as below:

How to apply (AI) technology to avoid vegetable, fresh fruit loss to global farmers' fresh vegetable , fruit excessive wastage loss increasing number when their crops growth process in global agricultural sector? (AI) will enable significant and valuable new solutions to avoid fresh crops, fruit, rice, vegetable food loss in their growing or irrigation process.

The internet of things (OIT) will assist (IA) in future intelligent agricultural systems, fuelled by large volumes of data acquired from images, videos and IOT sensors. For example, it be applied to water and sprays in agricultural sector. (AI) is smoothing the way for new levels of optimisation on our farms and across all horticultural activities. The automated irrigation systems are getting and the transporting of water to specific places. It is based on the real-time needs of plants. Moreover, (AI) techniques using IOT and sensors to analyse what's happening across many hectares of farming land in real time will enable improvements in predictive modelling.

Farmers will be able to check the advantages of specific phenotypes , or traits in certain growing over time . Predictive modelling will also help them forecast pest resurgences, dramatically preventing yield losses and reducing farmers' dependence on chemical pesticides to let vegetable, fruit, crop can be grown healthy.

For the university of Waikoto , NZ example, researchers are applying machine learning to near infra-red images of soil, meaning the soil does not have to be sent to the lab. This will enable farmers to apply fertilisers much more efficiently. Moreover, robots will be developed to roam between strains of needs. These bots are high enough that do not damage the soil, and because they release herbicides only onto the weeds. They are also doing more environmental protection behaviours. Many uses of (AI) in agriculture are focused on reducing the biological and ecological damage caused by inefficient use of pesticides.

For meet waste loss reducing aspect, (AI) technology can be applied to animal health monitoring . It can also be used to improve efficiencies in livestock management by optimising feeding and dispensing of medication. The (AI) technology can constantly monitor livestock , e.g. pigs, cows sheep animals movements, eating patterns and health and immediately flag animals that are showing unusual behaviour or reduced welling. They can then be treated quickly before they spread infection. So, farmers benefit is from cost reduction through more targeted use of antibiotics when also improving the treatment of livestock.

In the simplest terms, images are constantly captured and pre-processed through detection for frequency and density to livestock eating animals' eating behaviours and living and health conditions in order to provide health pork, beef, sheep meet to consumers to eat.

However, (AI) can be applied to crop seed or fruit improved growing or better irrigation aspect, for New Zealand kiwifruit agricultural irrigation case, yield well ahead of scheduled harvests. New Zealand kiwifruit growers have had to manually count fruit over certain areas and then to achieve the more accurate kiwifruit supplying number of consumers' demanding number scheduled harvests to satisfy New Zealand itself country's kiwifruit consumers' needs , even overseas kiwifruit consumers' needs. The agricultural sector would not know until the kiwifruit product hit supermarket shelves whether its spot sampling had been correct. Any miscalculation could cause kiwifruit waste loss. For example, if NZ kiwifruit farmers predict China kiwifruit consumer number will be on million kiwifruit consumer number in this year. However, they miscalculate the wrong kiwifruit supplying number either their needs are lesser. Then, it will occur shortage kiwifruit number to export to Chinese kiwifruit consumers in this year or their supplying export number are more, then it will occur excess kiwifruit number to Chinese kiwifruit consumers. So, (AI) technology can help NZ kiwifruit farmers to predict every country's kiwifruit needs in order to supply the enough kiwifruit number to every countries' supermarkets or fruit stores to sell. SO, it won't cause NZ kiwifruit excessive or shortage challenges occur more easily.

Hence, (AI) enabled technological tools can observant or supervise every countries' fruit consumers' eating habits to predict whether how many fruit number that they will need to eat every year more accurate. It is as simple as a smartphone to video along on trailers can help provide better estimates. The device videos , the orchard on –the-go and can then produce global fruit consumers' fruit eating habits to predict their fruit consumption behaviours more accurately in every year. From these video-based machine learning systems can detect more better and therefore count seeds and fruit months in advance. So, having these (AI) predictive crop or seeds growing number technology to predict whether is enough insights in advance would also enable harvesters to undertake section-based optimisation, improve food safety and direct fertiliser to specific locations. Global faming suppliers can better manage their crop , fruit seeds, vegetable seeds growing process and time to control or predict when they can be grown to sell when it can reaches the mature stage , even meat pricing and revenue forecasting with supermarkets or food or fruit store retailers accurately book shipping logistics and storage and reducing waste.

So, key (AI) technologies will extreme impact agriculture to change farmers' vegetable, fruit, tomato, potato, crop, and livestock animals feeding methods or behaviours to be improved better by machine learning, drones, computer vision. IOT robotics, satellite , data influence.

How to putting (AI) work in the vineyard for grape fruit growing better? For Lincoln Agri. Tech. a research and development company owned by Lincoln university , NZ case example, it is developing an (AI) solution which can make early season predictions of vineyard harvests. (AI) technology can help NZ grape growers and wineries to predict their grape yield each year. SO, (AI) technology can help them to do grape yield prediction work. A large number of manual workers do sample grape bunches work. SO, (AI) technology is working on creating a system that instead uses electronic sensors to accurately count grapes for NZ grape fruit farmers. The sensors will capture and analyse grape bunches within individual rows, and access the number, sizes and distribution, feeding these different kinds of grape number data into computer algorithms in order to predict grape yield at harvest time to calculate the different kinds of grape yield to different countries grape consumers' needs more accurately. New date will also be added to the (AI) computer system each year, leading to continuous improvements in the model's accuracy as more information is gathered under different conditions. Hence, (AI) system will enable NZ grape growers to accurately access differences in yield , not only between regions or vineyards, but also blocks and rows. Over the long term, site-specific grape yield prediction will help reduce costs by enabling better planning both in the vineyard and in NZ grape market, even overseas grape market both. This (AI) technology will benefit the agricultural industry by supporting better crop or seed management, smoother processing and fruit , vegetable, crop market based on capacity to supply the more accurate number.

Global farmers can apply (AI) technology to improve agricultural water system to let crop, fruit, vegetable to grow more easily to avoid waste loss number rises. Applying on farming sensors and other data to provide farmers with daily recommendations around nitrogen application and water and effluent irrigation . It can be accessed via smartphone, take the guess-work out of interpreting the large amounts of data farmers need to consider before making an irrigation decision.

(AI) agricultural water irrigation computer system can expand into nitrogen application management and water irrigation scheduling. Optimising the amount and timing of effluent are key components of ensuring farm sustainability and resource consent compliance, minimising leaching and optimising pasture growth.

Future (AI) technology just-in-time water management can provide enough water supply to satisfy agricultural fruit, vegetable, crop etc. food irrigation need to global different farming lands more easily. In farming industry, enough fresh water irrigation need is very important to influence any fruit , vegetable, crop etc. food growing process successfully. (AI) technology can be applied to this farming land water supply aspect. It can measure when the farming land needs how much water supply to provide to the farming land's fruit, vegetable, crop growth more easily. Either when the farming land does not need water supply, or when the farming land has still have enough water in the farming underground land. For example, a Florida water company is using artificial intelligence to reduce withdrawal of water from the area aquifer in Jacksonville, USA. Tis (AI) water supply measurement system can forecast water consumption , then monitors, regulates and adjusts supply in real-time , providing a just-in0time water supply to the farming underground lane. This minimises wall production during peak hours, optimises reservoir storage, and reduces the number of pump starts required, lowering energy consumption and maintenance costs.

The (AI) water supply management system can meet the fruit, vegetable crop growing demands of these food consumers needs and reduce the need to big new wells and preserve for un-predictive water supplying need for any fruit, vegetable, crop water need on any farming lands. So, every farming land will have accurate water supplying , it won't have excessive or shortage water supply challenge to every farming lands, if the country's farmers chose to use this (AI) water supply management system.

In the future, (AI) technology advantages to be applied to food waste aspect, it can influence: assisted farming to provide enough water supply to irrigate the most accurate and measured water to every farming underground lands to let any fruit, vegetable, crops' seeds to have enough water supply to grown rapidly, reducing open-sea fishing, considered use of farming land energy supply or affordable and clean energy supply.

In the future, artificial intelligence has the potential to let any fruit vegetable, crop seeds grow up successfully. It can be used to analyse seed genetic data to create crops that can thrive and adapt in any sudden changing environment or weather in order to keep the fruit, vegetable, crop seeds can still have large adapting effort to grow up in any bad conditions. It can increase effectiveness of food supply chains through the use of (AI) technologies to drive insights that improve any fruit, vegetable, crop growing up efficiency and reduce waste in any farm. It can also give recommendations to support for farmers to choose the best decision making in order to increase in productivity.

Instead of these , it can reduce the food loss in growing or manufacturing process. It can also help human to choose the healthcare diets. It includes to mine health care records to improve quality of treatments and provide better and faster health diets. It can analyse of large scale genetic data sets to help create new types of treatment and precision medicines customised for individuals, providing expert assistance in diagnosis especially in repetitive tasks, such as analysis of images and large bodies of research information, providing immediate first line consultation to improve waiting times to see a doctor, reducing pressure on frontline staff by using robots in healthcare, speeding up the development of new drugs allowing treatments to reach whose who need them more quickly, improving learning outcomes through the analysis of data about individual learning, social and learning contexts, and personal interests, providing virtual monitors for learning by integrating modelling, social simulation and knowledge representation, providing lifelong learning companions that help the learner to adapt and build new skills throughout their lifetime. Hence, it can bring the actual life knowledge to let food manufacturers, farmers and food consumers to learn how to avoid to do food wastage or food loss behaviours in our daily life experiences. Moreover, it can help farmers , food manufacturers to learn how to optimize energy generation and reduce environmental impact through analysis of operational and environment data as well as helping food consumers or food manufacturers to find the most affordable and clean energy in efficient ways od deals when they are cooking or manufacturing foods by using (AI) agents. Even, it can improve actions to fight climate change through better modelling and analysis of large or complex data sets in order to generate better insight to help to improve the sustainable management of land resources, e.g. soils, forest, biodiversity and allow greater understanding of the impact of better farming land use choices for fruit, vegetable, crops ' seeds growth through global agricultural industry development predictive analytic and machine learning.

In conclusion, based on above different (AI) technology predictive function s, so it explains why it can replace education method to avoid or reduce future good or energy shortage challenge more easily. It is due to food consumers or food manufacturers' food waste or loss behaviours which can not be controlled to avoided to cause easily in their food manufacturing or crop growing processes as well as food consumption processes. (AI) green data revolution will create a smarter, more flexible food waste controlling system as more data is created and shared between food supply chain partners and food consumers. It can bring positive benefits to agricultural industry, such as food factory manufacturing automation, intelligent food packaging, food waste or loss risk analytics in manufacturing processes , food supply chain number forecasting, food product personalisation and new avoiding food waste or loss ways of engaging with food consumers.

Finally, I shall discuss how (AI) technology can gather data to bring food waste or food loss threat consequent message to let humans (food consumers or food manufacturers) to understand how to change their eating waste habits or food manufacturing loss behaviours more easily as below:

Future (AI) technology can gather global food manufacturing and food consumption data to conclude one accurate food system trend model to let us to influence our negative or wrong eating habits or food manufacturing behaviours to improve to more positive in order to avoid food loss or food wastage causes easily.. The food eating or manufacturing behavioural system trends model can be as below:

It includes how to consider a number of trends that will influence the food system over the coming decade, focusing on small number of " key trends" in agricultural industry and supermarket, food stores, food grocery and food manufacturing industry, fishing industry, restaurant and hotel food supply industry, these trends which focus on a number of issues across the natural environmental, social and economic influences , due to future food waste or food loss consequent causes.

Changing social norms and working practices continue to influence the frequencey and format of food consumption. Predicting how the soical media influences to the way householders make food purchasing and dining decisions to influence food consumers' food waste behaviors from online. Predicting how the widening wealth gap and aging population are altering household food shopping and eating behaviours changes. Predicting explosion of data enabled technology concerns how the amount of data is growing at an predictive rate. The offers potential for a smarter, more responsive reducing or avoiding food waste behavioral system to food consumers or food manufacturers. Predictinv how the positive changes or influences of tackling major public health and environmental challenges are caused from humans (food consumers and food manufacturers) whose food waste or food loss behaviours. Predicting food system (big data gathering method) concerns food consumers or food manufacturers' frequency of food waste or food loss behavioural data to adatp to an uncertain operating environment as well as to find the methods how to fight the risks of climate related shocks to the food shortge challenge.

Hence, the (AI) data gathering aims to achieve these missions as below:

Learning how to grow in most technology is driven a revolution in how the entire food system operates from a better understanding of land resources to automated factories and kitchens. To bring data enabled technology that will be become cheaper and more accessible all the time, but the avoiding food waste system will fully capitalise on the benefits over tehe next ten years. This avoiding food waste system will be explored to companies, households and food waste policymakers seek to make better use of data. They include as below:

(1) Increasing number of devices connected to the internet and number of social media users to learn how to avoid to do food waste or food loss behaviours daily.

(2) Decreasing the cost of data storage technology and the size od data enabled devices.

(3) The food waste avoiding system can deal with th increasing complexity and sudden changing environmental , social and economic systems to avoid the failure to respond proactively to these new challenges to bring energy, water and food shortages consequences.

(4) Increaing efforts to fight the impacts of extreme weather events, agricultural pest ranges to the food avoiding waste system interconnectedness.

(5) Understanding how to increase soil health, crop diversity, global nutrition and quality and availability of water resources.

(6) Understanding how to fight climate change, it brings significantly affect the fruit, vegetable, crop's seed growth to the improved better in agricultural industry through its impact agricultural yields, agricultural food

changing prices influence, reliability of supply, food quality and food safety for ensuring long term food security and supply chain (food transportation process).

(7) Developments of the use of advanced monitoring agricultural systems to increase input efficiencies and anticipate food production risks, such as adverse weather.

(8) Skills for future food wastage or shortage challenges, learning how to fight climate change challenges.

In conclusion, (AI) preventive food wastage or shortage technological system will need to gather the data concerns when global climate and environement sudden change and finding anywhere the global most suitable farming lands are located in order to provide the right agricultural farming lands to let fruit, vegetable, crops' seed which can grow rapidly, finding anywhere the lands are located which have enough natural water supply in order to help us to solve food shortage challenge in order to irrigate enough water to farming lands to let agricultural foods grow more rapidly, and finding anywhere have enough weeds or food for pigs, cows, sheeps livestocks on the land to eat. So, above these are future (AI) preventive food wastage or shortage technological system will be invented to solve any one of these agricultural seeds growth and livestocks feeding challenges.

Factors influence householder energy consumption behavior

CHAPTER FOURTEEN

House quality influences householder electricity energy consumption behavior

Can artificial intelligence influence householder energy consumption behavior changing ? Can the house quality influence the householder electricity energy consumption or useful activities to be more or less. In general, house owners have both intentions for whose property. One intention is living the house by householder himself or herself or householder with families themselves. Another intention is that renting to others to receive rent income (landlord). So, in the housing market, the housing consumer includes either the property owner intents to rent to others to live for rent income aim or the property buyers intents to buy the house to be house owner to live. Does these both different property purchase intentions, which will influence the householder's attitude to use electricity energy consumption desire to be more or less, due to the householder's demand to whose house quality factor influence? This is one interesting question concerns the householder electricity energy consumption desire change to the householder, due to house's investment or house's living intention influences to house quality factor.

How does house quality factor influence to householder electricity energy consumption desire to be more or less? Has it relationship between house quality and house investment or living intention to cause house quality demand to influence the householder electricity energy consumption desire change or demand to be more or less? Has it relationship between regional housing market living or rent investment intentions, housing quality and electricity energy consumption more or less desire? I suppose that the determinants of the residential electricity energy demand form space-heating and cooking, due to the property quality demand influence and the householder's living or rent investment intention influence both, which will influence the householder's electricity energy consumption or useful behavior when he/she/they is/are living in the house.

I argue that rent properties are not only consumer goods, but it also constitute financial market assets. It is therefore reasonable to assume that rational (rent income investment intention) investors choose to raise housing quality (e.g. thermal insulation technological installing at home, heating or cooling technology or artificial intelligent window, lighting, door opening or closing) in order to attract many people choose to rent whose house to live. The householder's aim is to achieve an acceptable return on investment (ROI) or raising rent income aim when he/she rents whose house to anyone, it is easy to attract many people to choose to pay higher rent his/her house to live in the property rent market. Moreover, the another important factor is that rents and future house sale prices of properties differ regionally (or even locally), and largely depend on housing market fundamentals, such as either the house living buyer's income levels or the house rent buyer's income levels, vacancy rates, and/or householder investor's expectations.

Thus, if the householder expects to rent whose house and raises rent to attract many people choose to rent whose house to live, who will attempt to install many new technology in order to satisfy their high quality of life need when they can pay higher rent to rent to choose to rent whose houses to live. Their aim only achieves to raise housing quality, but any new technology will lead to increase electricity energy consumption or use in the house.

Hence, any high quality of houses will influence the householder to use or consume more electricity energy at home. It means that the householder will choose to consume or use more electricity energy at home, if he/she or the family householder demands to live more comfortable house and he/she/they can have high quality of living life at home. This comfortable living demand to the householder (property renter or property buyer) view point can explain why the better quality of house factor will influence the electricity energy consumption desire to the householder also to be more daily.

I shall indicate one home electricity energy consumption experiment, it indicated that utilizing aggregate data on regional space-heating energy consumption form over 300,000 apartment buildings in 97 German planning regions. The study applies structural equation modelling to estimate the influence of housing market fundamentals on the level of housing quality, and subsequently on regional electricity energy consumption. Consequently, it suggests that housing market fundamental explain regional differences in the housing quality.

In particular, findings show that the level of per capita income, investor' expectations about future housing market development as well as vacancy all explain regional differences in housing quality has a significant impact on electricity energy consumption.

In the way, this experiment can indicate evidence that regional housing market fundamental have a substantial influence on regional levels of housing quality and energy consumption desires to the German regional householders. This Germany regional householder experiment found important implications for high or low housing quality of the regional property building and householders either property living or property rent intention of comfortable living feeling need factor which will influence the regional property householder electricity energy consumption desire to be raised or reduced. These factors will influence the consequence of electricity energy demand to be increased or decreased needs every day for the regional householder as well as the country's electricity energy supplier(s) can gather the regional properties whether they are high or low quality to predict the regional properties householders' electricity energy consumption supply budget more accurate. It implies that an important determinant of residential housing quality will have possible to influence electricity energy demand to be more or less for long term. IN particular, this Germany regional residential experiment can explain and find an important role in formulating assumptions about the quality factor has chance to influence the regional residential future levels of electricity energy efficiency and consumption in the country. Hence, housing developments and electricity energy firms can follow this regional residential housing quality factor to evaluate whether the regional housing market is the corresponding investment patterns as well as the energy researchers can follow the regional residential housing quality whether it is high or low housing quality factor to evaluate the more accurate models of regional electricity energy demand to any regional residential householders' houses in the country.

In consumer behavioral view point, it explains that if the country government expected many householders feel to need to spend much electricity energy or have much electricity energy useful demand or desire at home. The country government ought to encourage the country residential property or house developers choose to build many houses which have technological product installed to satisfy the regional householders' residential comfortable living need when they choose the regions to build the high quality houses to let them to live. Then, the regional householders will be influenced to consume or use much electricity energy at homes, due to they feel that they are living at high quality and comfortable and high building technological installed apartments in the country's regions. Then, the country's government and electricity energy provider(s) may be raise much electricity energy efficiency and supply and profit , due to the regional residential householders' electricity energy consumption or useful desire need is therefore influenced to be more by the regional high quality of residential houses factor. So, the regional high quality of residential house factor will have relationship to the regional electricity energy consumption and efficiency to the regional householder's houses.

Otherwise, if the country government felt electricity energy is shortage, it ought encourage the property developers build many low quality and low building technological houses to let householders to live themselves or rent to others to live in the country's different regional residential development market. Due to the low quality of properties and low technological installed to properties factor which will influence any these different regional residential householders to choose method to solve shortage of electricity energy challenge to the country.

In conclusion, to apply consumer behavioral economic theory to property development market, if property quality factor can really influence the householder's electricity energy consumption desire to be used more or less at home daily. The country's property developers can apply this factor to predict property consumer individual property buying consumption behaviors more accurate. For example, if the US property developer planned to build low quality and low technological design buildings and lesser comfortable residential houses in the region in US. Then, its residential householder target will be trended the less acceptable of electricity energy consumption property buyers to choose to buy these regional properties to live in the US region because they can only accept to spend less electricity energy to use when they are living in the houses in order to save money daily. SO, the low quality , less comfortable and low technological installed design residential houses will satisfy their living needs. Otherwise, if the US property developer planned to build high quality and high technological installed design buildings and more comfortable residential houses in the region in US. Then, its residential householder target will be trended to the more acceptable of electricity energy consumption property buyers to choose to buy these regional properties to live in the US region because they can accept to spend more electricity energy to use when they are living in the houses in order to improve their living of quality. So, they wont's consider to spend more expenditure to use electricity energy for any technological products are installed in their properties in order to satisfy their comfortable living needs at their homes every day.

Consequently, property developers can attempt to gather marketing research concerns whether how many people who accept to use more electricity energy or use less electricity energy in order to predict they ought build how many high quality or low quality houses number in different regions more accurate in themselves countries or overseas countries property development market.

Environmental impacts of householder greenhouse gas electricity energy consumption activities

Can artificial intelligence influence householders accept to use greenhouse gas electrcity energy in preference? Can environment factor influence householder electricity energy consumption activities? Has environment factor relationship to influence householder electricity energy consumption behaviors? Socially, householder electricity energy consumption provides us with sources of living satisfaction , but if any sudden environment factor changes, whether it will influence householder consume or use more or less electricity energy decision at home. However, I assume householder electricity energy consumption will have a considerable proportion of the environmental impacts be influenced by our way of life and our economic decision of electricity energy consumption behavior.

What different environmental factors will influence householder electricity energy consumption decision? The external environmental factors include, for example, the country's electricity firms or government changes to electricity energy regulations, electricity energy production technologies change and business practices and government policies changing etc. different external environmental factors will influence any country's electricity energy consumption to householders' consumption desire to be more or less. It will also require changes to influence the householders to consume which kinds of electric products which are needed to be used in different electricity energy natural manufacturing resources.

Why does these external environmental factors impact householders' any behaviors to influence them to concern to use more or less electricity energy power or which kinds of electricity energy products choice at homes. How any why environmental factors impact will influence householder activities at home, such as electricity energy consumption and choice? What are the key components of external environmental factors influence householders' electricity energy consumption behaviors. I shall explain as below:

Firstly, we need to know whether what external environments are which can influence why and how householders need to change their activities to choose more or less or which kinds of energy power to be provided to them to use at home. Who is householder? Householder is an individual, family, or group of individuals living together as unit in a home. Consumption of electricity energy at home may be cooking food needs, needing have colder feeling to turn on fan or air condition at home in summer or needing have warm feeling to turn on heater at home in winter, watching television programs or listening music , playing computer games or used computers activities , reading activities and applying artificial intelligent technological tools to help householders to open or close homes' windows, doors etc. different home equipment which need to use electricity energy provisions. SO, their home activities need to turn on lighting electric tools , televisions, music machines, radios etc. different equipment which need to use electricity energy provision at home. SO, the purpose of householder consumption means consumption by individuals living in a household and it includes consumption both in and outside the home. Why does environmental impacts link to householders' electricity energy consumption? I shall focus on discussing of greenhouse gases (GHGS) energy product how any why it can influenced to householders to use.

The environmental impacts will influence this kind of greenhouse gases (GHGS) energy in the product lifecycle or delivery of the service to link the householder's energy consumption at home such as these several aspects:

Extraction and greenhouse gases production (supply number), physical distribution (delivery far long or close near short distance between the greenhouse gases manufacturing factory and the greenhouse gases supplier), resources consumed by marketing and retail activities (householder's needs to use the quantity of the greenhouse gases energy product), the greenhouse gases consumers search and purchasing activities(e.g. travel to shops, internet purchasing channel, , finding the which kinds of greenhouse gases products from internet, magazines, newspapers, radio advertisements etc. different medias,) , post-use greenhouse gases energy disposal (resale, reused or rubbish). The householder's physical behavioral impact environmental factor will influence how and why he/she chooses to consume greenhouse gases energy daily , e.g. impacts of a housing development, or a wind –farm that supplies greenhouse gases with power. So, the householder's greenhouse gases energy consumption behavior which will depend upon individual personal and subjective perspectives and value.

So, the householder's useful behavior or attitude of greenhouse gases energy product which will influence how he/she/ the family use or consume greenhouse gases energy, such as the householder individual environmental protection attitude which can impact how he/she/the family spends the quantity of greenhouse gases energy every day at home, if the householder does not expect our air or water or land is polluted , due to extraction of any natural gas resources to be manufactured any kinds of greenhouse gases products. Then, this environmental pollution issue will influence some householders choose to reduce to use more quantity of greenhouse gases products every day. Another environmental factors include the bio relates the (unsustainable) use of resources to avoid wasting much greenhouse gases energy to cause greenhouse gases energy supply shortage, avoiding the cause negative impacts of quality life , e.g. noise causing when the extraction of any natural resource from lands to the householder's house is near to the natural resource extraction land and health impacts, e.g. when the greenhouse gas householder user who often use the kind of greenhouse gas product when it is used to cook or heat any equipment to cause they to breathe dirty air at home often. These impacts can be measured in different ways include: monetary costs or loss, physical quantities of resources used or waste or pollution produced and the burden the greenhouse gases energy place on environmental resources. All of these external environment factors will impact the householder individual attitude or behavior how to use or consume greenhouse gases energy product at home.

All these environmental factors concern householder greenhouse gases energy consumer individual consumption attitude is influenced by environment pollution, greenhouse resource supply shortage challenge, greenhouse gases influence the householder's negative quality of life, negative health impacts, noise, waste money , raising economic cost to the householder which will impact whether how the householder choose to use the quantity of greenhouse gases product or the kinds of greenhouse gases products or other kinds of electricity energy products.

However, these are other external environmental factors which can impact how the householder decides to use greenhouse gas product at home. They include: the changes of energy regulation, e.g. the country government has quota number implementation to prohibit to import above the limited quantities of any kinds of greenhouse gas products to any countries. So, when the greenhouse gas energy supplying quantity is decreased, but if the country has may householders who need to buy different kinds of greenhouse gases products to be used at home. Then, the different kinds of import greenhouse gases energy products prices will be raised in possible, due to demand is more than supply in the country's greenhouse gas energy product market. Consequently, if the greenhouse gas energy price us risen above the general social acceptable level to the home greenhouse gas energy product householder consumers. Finally, it will influence them to choose to buy other kinds of gas energy products to replace the greenhouse gas energy product to use at home.

Another side, if the country's greenhouse gas energy manufacturing supplier sudden changes its greenhouse gas energy production technologies to choose to concentrate on manufacturing other kinds of energy products. Then, the greenhouse gas energy supply quantities will be only decreased, even future one day , it will cause greenhouse gas supply shortage challenge to let the country's home greenhouse gas householder consumers who can not buy enough quantity of any kinds of greenhouse gas energy products to satisfy their electricity needs at home every day. Consequently, when future on day , the country greenhouse gas energy manufacturer has none any quantity of greenhouse energy products to supply to the country's greenhouse energy householders to use at home. The, they must only choose other kinds of new energy products to replace the traditional useful greenhouse gas energy products to be used at homes.

In conclusions, these non-controlled external environmental factors can impact and influence the country's every householder consumer individual attitude or consumption behavioral change to how any why the country's householders either choose to buy much or less quantity of greenhouse gas products to use at home.

The effect of house space occupancy and building characteristics on householder electricity energy use

In general, society believes large space size occupancy house building characteristics factor which will influence householder use more energy at home, e.g. in summer, when the householder is living at the large space size occupancy house, who ought turn on all air conditions or fans at sleeping rooms or eating room or studying room. So, if the householder's house has two to three or more sleeping rooms. Then, he / she needs to buy more air conditions or fans in order to let all rooms' temperature to be fallen down to let he /she feel more cool comfortable feeling when the temperature is above 30 degree or more extreme hot in summer weather. Otherwise, when the temperature is low, e.g. between 0 degree to 10 degree or below 0 degree in winter weather. When the householder is living in one large space size occupancy appartment, which has thee to five sleeping rooms , even more and two studying rooms and one eating room, even more as well as every room has one heater. Then, he / she must turn on all heaters to let who to feel warm feeling when he / she is staying in the house. It brings these interesting questions.

Will large or small size space occupancy housing characteristics influence any householder often turn on heater or air condition or fan in whole house space occupancy area in order to the householder feels warmer or cooler feeling when he /she is staying in the house?

Has any space occupancy housing characteristics relationship to influence any householder to turn on heater or air condition or fan in whole house space occupancy area in order to the householder feels warmer or cooler feeling when he /she is staying in the house?

Does it bring positive relationship between turning on long time fan or air condition or heater and the house occupancy space characteristics is large or small size?

I shall attempt to give psychological evidences to explain the householder's house space occupancy area large or small size factor whether it can influence the householder choose to do long time or short time turning on heater or air condition or fan behavior in order to let he/she/the family to feel more cooler or warmer comfortable feeling when he/she/the family is staying in the house in summer or winter weather.

Does the house occupancy space size characteristics factor is the only one or important factor to influence the householder choose to turn on long or short time fan or air condition or heater in the house to let him/her/the family to feel more cooler or warmer comfortable feeling in summer or winter weather?

I feel that it is not exact right , due to the householder's house space occupancy size whether it is large or small characteristics to influence the householder choose to turn on long time or short time fan or air condition or heater time to let him /her/ the family to feel more cooler or warmer when he / she / the family is staying at home in summer or winter weather. The reason is because that the lifestyle of living quality need is different between developed countries and developing countries. The lifestyle of living quality factor will change the country's householder's expectation about the quality of living life. For example, for Africa, Korea, China , Japan, Hong Kong etc. developing countries. On the lifestyle of living quality need to these developing countries' householders aspect, that will cause a high environmental burden when they need to often turn on air conditions to satisfy more cooler feeling when they are staying at homes in summer or they need often to turn on heaters to satisfy more warmer feeling when they are staying at home in winter. Due to if their houses are large size space occupancy characteristics and they have more than at least two sleeping rooms and studying rooms and eating rooms and toilets number. Then, these householders who are developing countries' large space occupancy size characteristics houses, they won't like often turn on heaters long time to keep more warmer in their indoor whole space area in winter or they won't like often turn on air conditions or fans long time to keep more cooler in the their indoor whole space area house environment in summer .

The reason is possible because that the developing countries' householder chooses often to turn on their heaters or air conditions or fans long time in their houses when they are staying long time in their houses and their houses space occupancy sizes are very large, it will bring the electricity energy to be used more to these developing countries' householders' large space occupancy size characteristic houses. It means that the electricity fee will be also increased due to they often turn on heaters or air conditions or fans long time to keep their indoor temperature to be more cooler in summer or more warmer in winter. So, it seems that the developing countries' householders are living in the house whose space occupancy have very large size characteristics and more than two rooms house characteristics in the developing countries as above. Then, they won't often choose to turn on heaters or air conditions or fans long time to keep more cooler or warmer feeling in their house whole indoor space occupancy environment when they are often staying at home long time.

Their lifestyle of living comfortable feeling are lesser than the developed countries householders. Consequently, their lesser cooling or warming comfortable demand of living lifestyle factor will change their attitudes to use air conditions or fans or heaters turning on time in order to limit heaters or air conditions or fans turning on time to be shorter than the developed countries houeholders' heaters or air conditions or fans turning on time at homes. Due to the long time turnong on air conditions, fans , heaters at the developing countries' householders' homes, it will cause to spend much electricity energy to lead electricity fee charges to be raised to the developing countries' householders ' homes when they are often staying at homes in summer or winter weather. Hence, the house space occupancy large size characteristics ought not influence the developing countries householders choose to turn on air conditions , fans or heaters long time in order to let them to feel more cooler or warmer at homes in summer or winter weather.

So, the developing countries' house space occupancy large size characteristics householders won't be more acceptable to pay higher electricity energy fee when they are staying at homes at summer or winter weather. Due to they do not often choose to turn on heaters, air conditions or fans long time during they are staying at homes. Otherwise, the developed countries, e.g. UK, UK , France, Germany, Swiss, Singapore, Italy etc. countries. In general, these developed countries' householders' living lifestyle quality needs are higher than the developing countries. So, when the summer or winter weather is coming, if the temperature is extreme cold, e.g. below than 0 degree or it is extreme hot, e.g. higher than 30 degee.

Then these developed countries' householders will easy accept to turn on air conditions or fans or heaters long time at home in order to keep their appartment in door temperature to be more cooler in extreme hot in door environment or more warmer in extreme cold in door environment when these developed countries' householders are often staying at homes long time at night after their day time working time or schooling time. Because these developed counties' householders' quality of living lifestyle needs or demands are higher than the developing countries' householders. So, they won't consider that they will pay more electricity fee , due to they often turn on air conditions, fans or heaters long time to let them to feel more comfortable in cooler or warmer indoor large size space occupancy environment. So, it seems that the electricity energy efficiency will be raised to the developed countries' householders who are living in the house space occupancy large size characteristics and they will be possible to pay more electricity fees during they are often staying at home in extreme hot summer or extreme cold winter weather. In conclusion, due to the living lifestyle quality need (demand) is different between the developed countries' householders and the developing countries' householders. It will influence the householders' long time or short time spending time on air conditions or fans or heaters indoor space occupancy size characteristics environment in order to achieve more cooler or more warmer feeling in their houses. Consequently, the long or short time of turning on air conditions, fans, heaters for the developed or developing countries householders' activities factor will be more influential to compare the house space occupancy large or small size characteristics factor to influence their cooler or warmer feeling in their houses. SO, the house indoor environment electricity energy consumption efficiency degree to the developing or developed countries' every householder house in summer or winter to the developing or developed householders in summer or winter weather , which is more influenced by the living lifestyle qualty factor to the either developed countries or developing countries householders. Hence, any developed or developing countries' electricity suppliers need to consider the building areas of property development market buyers their living style quality demands (needs) whether their living style quality demands are higher or lesser than the other building areas of property development market, they ought not consider whether the building locations of the houses' space occupation sizes whether they are large or small sizes in order to evaluate the householders will live at the building areas of property development locations ,whose electricty energy spending efficiency more accurate.

How to help low income household earners to reduce not essential electricity energy expenditure spending at homes

Has it relationship between the householder income and the electricity energy needs? How to evaluate the subsidies and social tariffs to assist lower income earners to analyze household energy consumption more accurate?

Electricity energy is essential needs for every householder at home, e.g. lighting, cooking power, healthcare, sanitation, cooler or warmer temperature indoor control at home. However, for lower income household earners, it its burden when they need often to use electricity energy to supply power to any home electricity tools to do any acticities at homes. If any these countries' lower income householder earner target can not get the reasonable subsidies to assist them to solve any electricity energy tools' electricity energy poer needs. Due to their lower income leve, it is possible that to knfluence them have enough electricity supply to help them to use to cook rice and food and vegatabe to eat, boil water to drink, turning on light tools to help them to read, watch TV, listen radio, music any entertainment or essential needs at homes at night or morning afternoon time. These lower income household earners will be easy to sick , due to they have no enough electricity supply to help them to use use electric bottles to boil water or cook food to eat. Then they only drink not boiled water or not cooked food to eat at homes in possible, due to they have no enough income to pay electricity fees every month.

Hence, how to evaluate the lower income household earners' electricity fee need (demand) level in order to provide the reasonable subsidies amount to assist every country's low income household earner to help them to pay the reasonable electricity fee which is one important issue to every country's government today. It brings this question: How to evaluate or analyze or predict every lower income household individual or family earner's every month electricity energy demand (need) more accurate?

It is one essential issue to be value to consider to every country's government. Moreover, to the estent that energy subsidies must be essential to be provided by public sources to all low income household earners or that a social tariff may be designed for improving access to energy for certain low income social earner groups. Hence, how to structure the energy subsidies between energy and income levels to be better target, such public mechanisms, and to avoid regressive subsidies unfairly. For example, India and China these both countries' income poverty and energy poverty population are the large number. So , these both countries' governments need to focuse on more aggregated effects and analyze the effects of rural electrification at the local level on the decrease in energy poverty in rural low income poverty and energy poverty householders. Therefore, every country government needs to point regressivity of the subsidy for electricity. There is room to analyze to what extent low income household earners along the income distribution demand some forms of energy, and to suggest better and fair low income targeting household earners energy subsidies supply policies.

Each government does not only consider energy issues from a social point of view, it also needs have a manner to consider a possible link between energy, hunger reduction, and food security for each country's low income household earners group. So, every government has responsibility to calculate the determinants of different sources of energy consumption at the low income houehold earner level for urban and rural both populations in order to evaluate the electricity subsidies and to test whether every low income householder earner characteristics plays a role in determining energy consumption.

In general, in the use of energy measured as that for cooking, such as LPG reduces the exposure of households to hazardous, increases the consumption of different types of foods and medicines, improves the distribution of time between household memners, enables studys with more light, reduces the use of digital computer entertainment tools at home, and moderates the use of wood as fuel, preventing deforestation. These methods are the best suggestions to help low income householder earner groups to reduce time to use electricity at homes. When they spend less time to use electricity to do any not essential activities, e.g. watching television, playing electric games from home computers, listening music. They only use electricity to turn on light read, to turn on rice cooker to cook, when they feel hungey to eat. Then, I believe that these social low income household earner groups will reduce to pay much not essential electricity energy expenditure at homes. Hence, every country government ought need to persuade low income household earners to avoid to use electricity to do any not essential activities in order to raise electricity energy consumption in long term time.

It will bring less amount of energy subsidies expenditure benefits to every country's government. Hence, the success to persuade any countries' low income household earners to reduce to spend much time to do any electric entertainment activities of consumption behaviors at homes often. This is the most efficient and the most successful energy subsidiary method to help them to reduce electricity energy expenditure when they are staying at homes. Hence, if any country government expected the low income household earners can continue really reduce electricity energy expenditure, they need to learn to do the meaning essential activities which are needed to use electricity at home habitally. Then, they can change their electricity useful entertainment living habit, e.g. using computers to play games, listening music, watching television entertainment habits at homes to cause essential daily needs of electricity useful living habit, e.f. using cookers to cook rice or cook food to eat, turning on lights to read , turning on heaters to bath, turning on air conditions to keep cool temperature or turning on heaters to keep warm temperature at homes.

Consequently, they won't need to pay much electricity expenditure at home, due to their waste useful electricity entetainment living habits have changed to do any essential useful electricity activities at homes.

Another kind of method to reduce the determinants of energy demand to the low income householder earners. The governments can persuade them to consider the variation factor can influence their electricity energy expenditure are increased or decreased at homes. It is not the electricity or gas price is increased from the electricity suppliers. It is that their bad living habits of waste electricity or gas to do any not essential activities at homes. e.g. the householder often turn on light tools to read or listen music or watch television in whole night, he/she ought need to sleep at night, but he/she does not go to bed to sleep in whole night. He/she chooses to turn on light to do these activities. Then, he/she will waste much electricity at whole night. Also, some householders like to bath more than half hour, even one hour, when it is winter, they need to turn on heaters to provide electricity to cause the bath room has warm water to provide to them to bath, Their long time bathing behaviors will be also waste electricity or gas energy from long time heating in bath rooms. So, they need to change their waste electricity consumption living behaviors at homes.

So, I suggest that some low income household earners will need to be taught to change their bad using electricity enery living habits from governments' public relation promotion in order to change the low income household earners' bad or incorrected useful electricity or gas living attitude to achieve and to avoid them often to do electricity or gas energy waste behaviors at homes. So, different countries' governments need to teach them how to do the correct or right electricty or gas useful activities (living habits) or let them know or feel how to use their electricity or gas which can help them to reduce to waste the not essential extra electricity or gas energy. Consequently, they must reduce electricity or gas expenditure as well as electricity or gas shortage challenge won't be caused by their electricity or gas useful waste behaviors (activities) at homes.

In conclusion, energy subsidies method is not the best solution to help low income household earners to reduce to use electricity or gas energy. Because it is only short term benefit to reduce their electricity or gas expenditure at homes. The best solution is that to let them to know or feel why and how they have responsibilities to change their incorrent or wrong electricity or gas consumption bad habits in order to avoid global electricity or gas energy is waste to be used, even it is caused shortage from householders' energy waste behaviors.

Factors influence householder energy efficient consumption behaviors at homes

What factors can influence householders how to use energy in efficient way at homes. It depends on different countries householders' living habits to cause their choices to use energy efficiently at homes. In general, global householders energy every day consumption or use aims include cooking, heating, and cooling or warming rooms, lighting , water-boiled use and computer playing games entertainment etc. activities at homes every day. Some activities are often essential at homes, e.g. cooking, cooling or warming temperature in rooms, lighting , water-boiled use. So, their activities must not avoid to use energy at homes often. Otherwise, some activities are not essential at homes, e.g. playing entertainment games from computers, cooling rooms in summer, listening music, watching television etc. these activities. The householder can choose either to use energy to turn on these equipment tools or not to do these non essential activities at homes often. In general, householders rely on energy to make ourselves lives comfortable, productive and enjoyable. However, global householders need to learn how we can use energy resources wisely because global every householder has responsibility to manage resources includes: reducing total energy use and using energy more efficiently in order to avoid energy shortage crise occurrence. The choices are make about how we use energy, e.g. turning machines off when not in use of choosing to buy energy efficieny appliances will have increasing impacts on the quality of our environment and lives.

Energy conservation includes any behavior that results in the use of less energy. Energy efficiency involves the use of technology that requires less energy to perform the same function. For example, a compact fluorescent light buld that uses less energy to produce the same amount of light as an incandescent light buib is an example of energy efficiency. So, a householder's decision to place an incanadescent light bulb with compact fluorescent is an example of energy conservation. So, as individuals, every countries' householder choices and actions can result in a significant reduction in the amount of energy used in each sector of the economy.

So, I bring this interesting question: What factors can influence householder to choose to do any efficient energy consumption or useful behaviors at homes? I believe every countries' householders will have their different living attitudes and their living attitudes can influence their behaviors or activities to choose hoe to use energy at home. I shall indicate some countries' householders' living attitudes to explain the factors can influence them to use energy efficiency at homes as below:

● Is the low income and rising price of modern fuels both factors best to influence Nigeria householders choose to use energy efficiently?

Firstly, for Nigeria householders energy consumption habit at homes example, it is richly with natural resources, modern energy resources which provide many householders with biomass (mostly firewood) and some other householders modern energy sources, such as kevosene, liquefied, petroleum, gas and electricity for their use. So, it is one country which can manufacture to provide energy for itself to use. It doesn't need to depend on other countries to import any kinds of energy to householders to buy to use at homes. But, it has social challenge, the poverty problem in Nigeria goes beyond low income, savings and growth rate, due to its low level of education, poor governamce, high level of unemployment factors influence.

It is important to know how Nigeria householders meet their basic energy needs between poverty and energy can bde described in terms of quality and quantity of energy used. Generally, most poor householders use biomass fuels because of affordability and they (householders) do not have energy equipment (such as, gas cookers, electric cookers etc.) . So, it seems Nigeria householders won't demand their living quality to be improved. It implies that they will use any kinds of energy efficiently at homes, e.g. gas, electricity, due to they find themselves in energy poverty. Although, this country has enough nature resources to manufacture energy to provide to householders to use, but due to many people are low income group, so they won't spend too much expenditure to buy much energy to use at homes. So, the rising prices of modern fuels, such as liquefied, petroleum , gas (LPG) and electricity and their erratic supply have made many householders revert to the use of traditional fuel, such as firewood and charcoal.

It brings this questions: Is the low income and rising price of modern fuels both factors best to influence Nigeria householders choose to use energy efficiently?

The hypothes is predicated on the economic theory of consumer behavior. However, when income increases, householders not only consume more of the same goods, they also need higher quality . So, it applies economic theory to householder's energy consumption behavior at home. It explains why low living standards induce greater dependence on firewood and other biomass fuels owing to a combination of income and substitution effects, such as Nigeria low income household energy home users case. it explains why Nigeria householders can accept to use firewood and charaval traditional energy to replace liquefied, petroleum , gas (LPG) and electricity modern energy . So, economic theory explains the Nigeria household energy users why they can accept to use traditional energy to replace modern energy and their energy useful or consumption behaviors are efficient at homes. Although, Nigeria has enough natural resource to manufacture modern energy to supply to householders to use at homes. But, due to these modern energy products prices are raised to the price level of householders who can not accept. it causes to Nigeria householders only choose to buy the cheap biomass, firewoods to replace high price of modern energy products to use at home often. So, they can accept their quality of living to be fallen down. So, expensive modern energy product price is one factor to influence some countries' householders to choose to buy cheap traditional poor quality of nature energy, e.g. firewood or biomass, to use at homes. Hence, they can raise energy efficiency to use when they choose to use traditional nature energy to replace modern nature energy at homes.

● Does season factor influence New Zealand householders' energy consumption behaviors at homes

Secondly, for New Zealand householders energy consumption habits at homes , for example, their living quality needs are general comfortable need feeling. Their countries' houses of space heating was found to average 34% of total housholder energy use. The relation to space heating includes low indirect temperature are associated with persistent under-heating , whether some space heating sources tend to be higher or lower in winter indoor temperature than others and winter indoor temperatures are compared to international benchmarks and established healthy temperature ranges. So, New Zealand occupant's perceptions of winter indoor temperature conditions are presented and explored in relation to heating patterns and household energy consumption. So, it seems that NZ winter temperature is low. Moreover, it will influence householders need to turn on heaters to keep more warmer feeling indoor. Then, they will use more electricity energy. In special, if the householders' houses spaces are large sizes . Hence, their heaters need long time to keep whole houses' areas or spaces or rooms temperature to be rised up in order to let they do not feel very cold in winter. So, NZ's winter extreme cold weather will influence householders' energy use or consumption to be increased in winter.

The electricity efficiency to every NZ householder is very high in winter to compare spring, summer, autumn seasons. Hence, if NZ electricity suppliers expected to forecast electricity consumption more accurate in NZ. In order to ease the life for both electric net designers and electricity suppliers, it was decided to find out, how the NZ weather conditions and every householder's house space size factors to influence the power consumption to NZ householders. If there is a clear trend observed , then this relation can be used for power consumption forecasts to NZ householders.

Why does NZ weather condition factor and householder's house space size factor can predict householders' electricity consumption at homes. Due to geographic location on the global the lowest south sets specific conditions for weather, such as NZ's south island geographic location is near to south ocean in our earth. It is a country where average annual temperatures are well between 10 degree to below 10 degree at NZ south island special geographic location to near to the sourth ocean in our earth at the same time.

However, large part of mankind is living in the conditions where there are four different seasons in NZ geographic location, dark winter, which is cold and snowy, spring with rising temperature and high precipitation, sunny , dry and rather hot summer, and windy and wet autumn. These conditions lead to different patterns in electric appliances use in NZ householders, in special, in NZ south island householders. If trends in electric energy use have substantial correlation with weather conditions, this can help NZ electric energy suppliers and producers to forecast electricity consumption and thus organize and manage production of electric energy.

Consequently, it will lead to much more stability in energy supply to NZ every householder. For example, when the

NZ energy supplier gathers data concerns every householder's house space size data, e.g. the house has how many sleeping rooms, toilets, bath rooms, eating rooms and reading rooms number, even the house has how many family members are living in every NZ geographical location. Then if it can follow different location of NZ houses spaces sizes whether they are large or small space size as well as whethe every house has how many family members are living to evaluate whether how much electricity efficiency can satisfy their comfortable living needs in winter. Then, it can evaluate whether they will use how much electricity efficiency for their needs in different seasons. If in winter, many householders are living in the large space size house in the geographic location. Then, it is possible that the geographic location is householders will use much electricity efficiency and where geographic location hosueholders who will be possible to pay the most highest electricity fee to compare the other geographic location of small space size of house householders. Hence, weather factor is the most influential to change NZ householders ' electricity energy consumption behaviors at homes.

● Urbanization level and income per capita both tangible factors as well as temperature (weather variation factor) will have close relationship to influence China householder energy consumption or useful needs at home every day For China householder energy consumption habit example, what factors can determine to impact this country's householders energy useful behavior at homes? Can the impacts of these factors be quntified? What are China householder energy consumption trends and characteristics? I shall explan as below:

I believe the influential factors include these three aspects to China householder energy users: Income per capita, urbanization level an annual average temperature (weather). These factors will influence any China householder energy useful or consumption behavior at homes.

Temperature (weather variation factor) is intangible from eastern region to western region of Chin, variances largely depend upon economic level and the provincial level. So, some regions were warmer and cooler temperature will influence the regional China householder how to use electricity. In addition, th influence of urbanization level varies according to income level as well as the urbanization level has more significant impact on the structure and efficiency of China householder energy consumption thatn on its quantity. So, the urbanization level and income per capita both tangible factors will have close relationship to influence China householder energy consumption or useful needs at home every day. Moreover, these two tangible factors (urbanization level and income per capita both factors) have the more influential to impact China any one of household family energy consumption or useful habit to compare temperature factor at home. Because temperature can only influence than to choose to turn on heaters to keep more cooler in summer or turn on air conditions (fans) to keep more warmer in winter.

The electricity energy needs for these equpoment tools which will be influenced less. Otherwise, the urbanization level and income per family householder how to choose to spend more or less electricity or gas etc. energy at homes. Because in behavioral economy view point, when individual householder has more income and the urban in the China geographic location is lising many high income and high household families memebrs to every house. Then, the urbanization household energy household enery useful or consumption level will be raised. Such as China household electricity users case, e.g. large cities have many high income and many houses have more than four families members to live on one house together. Then, the electricity or gas energy efficiency will be influenced to rise. The city urbanization and per capita income level is high to these large cities have high to income population, who are living in these cities in China.

Moreover, the impact of lifestyle on energy use mainly reflects types and purposes of fuels are chosen by different China households factor which will influence the urbanization level of energy choice use. China is a country with typical binary economics and social diversity and these is significant difference in the consumption pattern between urban and rural regions. Urban residents consume high-quality energy, such as electricity, natural gas , heating power, solar energy and gasoline. For rural residents, usually use coal, and bismass energy because they are cheaper price energy products which requires much time and labor and are heavy indoor pollutants . The difference in energy consumption pattern between urban and rural China residents is closely related related to living of quality needs, building structure, e.g. steel or stone etc. different materials, manufacture, easily access clean and effective feels through the electric grid, natural gas network and district heating systems.

Therefore, it explains why urbanization level is as an integrated variable reflecting social progress situation to influence urban and rural regions, such as large cities , small cities and rural countryside regions' household energy consumption or useful behaviors which have differnet kinds of fuel useful demands and energy efficiencies qualify and quantity demand, or needs at homes. Consequently, it explains, urbanization level and income per captia level both factors are more influential to China household energy consumption at home to compare temperature (weather , seasonal) factor.

● Employment rates or gross domestic product macro economic variation factor, residential space size factor, and the government's implementation of energy labeling schemes provide significant impacts on Taiwan residential electricity consumption .

For Taiwan householder electricity consumption characteristics in the residential sector, which has different factors and pattern to compare China householder electricity householder electricity consumption habit at home. Although, they are the same Asia country. I shall explain these reasons as below:

For Taiwan electricity householder factors influence their energy useful or consumption behaviors at homes. The main factors can influence their electricity energy useful patterns include: employment rates or gross domestic product macro economic variation factor, residential space size factor, and the government's implementation of energy labeling schemes provide significant impacts on Taiwan residential electricity consumption . However, the impacts of electricity raising price and the energy supply reducing shortage efficiency standards do not significant to influence the Taiwan residential electricity consumption behavior at sources.

It means that it won't influence Taiwan householders to use electricity or gas or any kinds of energy number to be reduced, even the Taiwan government energy suppliers sudden raise, any kinds of energy price and reduce to supply energy to satisfy Taiwan householders daily essential needs at homes.

In fact, Taiwan had improved gross domestic product (GDP) and it had raised employment rates recently. So, many Taiwanese has jobs to work, due to Taiwan economy had improved to be better. So, growth had also raised. The economy improvement causes many Taiwanese had enough jobs to work, due to new businesses are set up. Many consumers excit any kinds of businesses are invested to Taiwan from overseas or local investors. So, consumption is grown, the electricity consuming applicances are selected, as the household consumer focus grousp number if also influenced to be increased. So, Taiwan economy had improved to be better, it will encourage many electricity consuming applicances products are encouraged to excited to be selected to seel in Taiwan. Due to many different kinds of electricity consuming appliances are supplied to attract Taiwanese to choose to buy to bring to their homes for cooking, boiling water, or keeping rooms to be cooler or warmer temperature confortable feeling intention in winter or summer seasons. So, these electricity consuming appliances, e.g. rice cookers, heaters, air conditions, fans, bathing gas heaters etc. different home electricity consuming appliances will be increased to supply to satisfy Taiwan householders' needs. When they decide to buy any news electricity consuming applicances to bring to homes to use.

● Environment scientists' education message how to influence Greece householders home energy consumption behaviors from primary energy to change secondary energy

Finally , I shall indicate Greece, this western which will influence this country's householders have desires to do household energy conservation patterns or conservation energy consumption behaviors or energy conservation activities at homes. I shall explain the social economic variable, such as consumers' income and family size variation factor which can influence the different Greece family household members differences towards energy conservation preferences. IN addition, the variable, such as environmental information feedback and consciousness of energy problems are characteristics of the energy saver consumer.

Why and how can environmental pollution , environmental protection, energy conservation information message can influence Greece householders to choose to do energy use consumption conservation or less energy useful behaviors at homes. It is one interesting energy efficient use behaviors , due to Greece householders are influenced by energy conservation or environmental protection message.

In fact, scientists agree overconsumption of natural resources is a major threat to oue lives in earth. Environmental problems like greenhouse effect, ozone layer depletion, and acid rain effect are not any more problems of a specific region or environmental problem. Also, economic theory is indicated that in order to gain comfort and time households are becoming excessive energy users, neglecting the environmental impact of their choices.

Environment scientists bring these environment pollution message to influence Greeks (Greece householders) to change their energy consumption behaviors at homes. The environment scientists' message indicate that we are facing global warmth and natural resource and energy shortage challenges. Due to our Earth have limited natural resource numbers to supply to us to manufacture energy, but global population has been increasing every year. Thus, it is possible that we have energy shortage crisis. Also, manufactures are spending too much energy to waste to manufacture any products, the energy will cause air or water pollution in manufacturing process or drivers are driving their vehicles to pollute air on the roads.

Hence, environment scientists' message influence Greece householders began to consider these questions concern to reduce fossil fuel energy. Why do we need to Safety in using fuel and handle gas leaks? Why do we feel town gas smell? How is electricity located at electric station far away from town area? How to solve problems caused by the use of fossil fuels? How to reduce the use of fossil fuels?

Greece householders consider to solve the problems, the best way is to reduce thir used of fossil fuel. This helps prevent fossil fuels form being used up too quickly. Also, it helps them to reduce environmental problems because fewer pollutants are given out when less fossil fuels are used. Can human help to reduce the use of fossil fuels? Fossil fuels are mainly in power station. Although they use some fossil fuels for our gas cooker and car, it won't make much difference if I use less. Fossil fuel is not used renew primary energy. Most of energy Greece householders use come from fossil fuels, for example, the electricity we use is generated in power stations by burning fossil fuels. The buses they ride use diesel oil. Therefore, they can help reduce the use of fossil fuels by saving energy in Greece daily lives.

The actions that Greece householders can take such as: setting the air-conditioner to a higher temperature, walking instead of using lift, taking a short shower instead of a bath. This reduces the use of the hot water and thus the energy needed to heat the water. Thus, many people can help a lot to reduce our use of fossil fuels to avoid fossil fuel shortage risk occurrence.

Greeks (Greece householders) had been beginning to conern that they will face energy shortage challenge if they can not adopt more energy conservation actions. Because the Greece government began to bring negative environmental pollution and energy shortage challenge message if they often waste to use any kinds of energy, e.g. electricity , gas excessive number efficiency at homes. Then, they will be possible to fac energy shortage and environmental pollution challenge to their country in future one day. So, this energy shortage and environment pollution message has bring predictive negative worries to influence many Greece householder energy home users choose to reduce to avoid the waste of any kinds of energy use at homes.

So, their reducing energy use actions that had encouraged them to cause habits to avoid to waste excess energy to do any non essential electric appliances useful or consumption activities at homes often. Moreover, the environment protection and energy conservation message has changed many Greece householder to make decision and activities to change their lifestyle to b low living quality from high living quality. So, the environment protection and energy conservation message factor has much influential to change Greece household energy users' daily energy conservation or less energy use consumption activities at homes.

Greeks feel greenhouse energy can be environmental protection enegy. A greenhouse can trap heat in the sunlight and keeps the air inside the greenhouse warm enough for plants to grow. The glass roof and walls of a greenhouse let in sunlight but prevent heat from escape, this makes the greenhouse warm inside. Similarly, some gases in the Earth's atmosphere can trap heat from the sun and keep the Earth warm. This is called the greenhouse effect. The gases energy that can trap heat from the sun are called greenhouse gases. It is future one kind of potential primary energy to reduce environmental pollution new energy products for human consuming. So, environmental protection message influence them to consume greenhouse enegy at homes.

So, environment scientists' environment pollution message had influence Greece householders concern to apply seconday energy (environment protection) to replace electricity energy to use at home. They will change energy to use at home. The scientists' messages have more influential Greece householders energy change consumption behaviors at homes. The messages are as below:

There are different forms of energy, e.g. light, heat, sound, wind, water, electrical kinetic, chemical and potential energy. Some form energy is primary energy and it can not renew to use, e.g. light, sound, wind, water, fossil fuel etc. Some form energy is secondary energy and it can renew to use in possible, e.g. nuclear, electric charge battery etc. Why does human need to concern how to manufacture secondary energy? Because it is possible that our natural resource will be consumed all, thus we will face primary energy shortage risk. If human can invent any new form of man-made secondary energy to renew to use in order to avoid primary energy shortage to supply to use to use, then human won't only depend on our Earth natural resource energy supply numbers. We can invent any new secondary energy to renew to use again either replaces primary energy or instead of primary energy limit number supply.

What is energy change? For television energy change power case. Firstly, electrical energy changes to television power to be used by television itself, then it changes to light power, next it changes to light power. How to choose fuel form to use? Due to energy can change to different form of powers to supply different form of power advantages to supply to human to use, so it is possible that we can also invent any secondary man made renew used energy to change different form powers to supply us to use, e.g. nuclear energy changes to light or sound or heat form of powers ; electrical charge batteries changes to light or sound or heat form powers to satisfy our daily life needs.

The environment scientists' energy consumption education influence Greece householders concern how to change to use secondary energy to replace primary energy at homes as below:

For primary natural resource fuel energy example, different fuel has different feature, e.g. easy to burn, safe to use, gives out a lot of energy, inexpensive, produces little air pollution, easy to transport and store. How can we use in different channels, such as heating food, hot pat, driving vehicles.

For example, although coal is not expensive to cause electricity energy for past transportation tool, e.g. traditional coal energy train or our daily home cooking, but it has negative influence to environment air pollution. Hence, we ought to follow the primary natural resource energy's feature to decide how to apply what aspects of our life needs.

For example, if the country's people hope to reduce pollution when who use any kind of energy, e.g. US , Europe energy markets. The energy entrepreneur ought concentrate on manufacturing the kind of energy which can reduce environment pollution to be the least level to supply the country people to use, e.g. electric charge battery supplies to these countries' drivers to drive their vehicles on the roads, wind energy or water energy to manufacture electricity power supply to reduce air or water pollution ; or if the country people hope to buy the inexpensive energy to use, even the energy's quality and performance is worse, e.g. China, India, Hong Kong markets. The energy entrepreneur ought concentrate on manufacturing the lowest cost and enough supply of natural resource to manufacture the kind of energy to sell cheap price to these countries to use, e.g. China, Africa can accept to use e.g. gas, coal, fuel energy to use to compare developed countries people, e.g. UK, US; or if the countries people who hope to use energy which can easy to transport and store, e.g. light coal. The energy entrepreneur can choose to concentrate on manufacturing much coal to supply to the countries people to use, e.g. China, Arica Thus, to choose to manufacture which kinds of energy supply to the countries market people to use, the energy entrepreneur how decides to manufacture which kind of energy, it depends on which kinds of fuel advantages of the countries people most concerning.

What is energy meaning? It is defined a dynamic quality, it is a fundamental entity of nature that is transferred between parts of a system in the production of physical change within the system, and it is usually regarded as the capacity for doing work, and it is usable power (such as heat or electricity) or the resources for producing such power.

Why does secondary energy own investment worth? Because the different forms of primary natural resource energy will have supply shortage crisis, such as natural resources coal, gas, solar, wind, water, geothermal, biomass(organic material) etc. However, human can attempt to explore any undiscovered Earth or Space resource to manufacture any kinds of secondary energies, e.g. nuclear energy, electric recharge battery energy to supply to electric vehicle or space robots transportation tools to use or satisfy our daily life needs in future one day. So any kind of undiscovered secondary man-made renewed used energy resources have potential commercial worth to any energy entrepreneurs, it is possible that they can replace traditional primary energy to supply to human to use for our different aspects of life needs. In the future, the secondary energy demand will increase, when primary energy supply number has decreased form natural exploration. So, it will cause the effect of any demand of secondary energy product to be raised and prices to be increased in possible. Due to global population has been growing up, considerably China and India both countries populations have been increasing rapidly. Scientists predict there are more than 1.2 billion people worldwide will lack access to electricity, and more than 2.5 billion still use wood, charcoal to cook and heat in the future when primary energy has no enough number to supply to us to use. Hence, the fact that demand is this much greater than supply to make energy a prime market for further growth.

Although, secondary energy will have much investment worth, but energy like all other investments will carry risks. The internal and external risk factors include such as: policy is always changing to prohibit which do energy trading more easily between the energy exporting and importing countries, the secondary energy manufacturer itself own abilities to invent and to manufacture any kinds of secondary energy, improved technology can quickly make an technology obsolete, geopolitical rifts can happen overnight, the country's energy consumer (user)'s preferable choice to use which either kinds of secondary energy or secondary energy. So, it seems that (man-made) renewed used secondary energy industry can provide above-average returns, but it can also bring high risk commercial investment.

Traditionally, energy supply companies will apply those methods to operate energy providing businesses. For Shell,. Exxon examples, which had own gas stations, explore and drill for gas on their own. Other companies specialize in a part of the energy market, e.g. leasing oil rigs for example, or operating a pipeline. Energy supplying companies can choose to manufacture any kinds of energy to supply, e.g. trade oil, gas, coal, uranium, electricity etc. Any energy price and supply is demanded on the countries energy users' which kinds of energy most choice need or certain energy commodities to be chose to use popularly. For example, if US most people prefer to use secondary man-made renew used energy more than primary energy. Then, US energy manufacturers ought concentrate on manufacturing much different kinds of secondary man-made renew used energy to prepare to supply to its domestic US market in order to raise secondary energy price to sell in its country. So, the energy manufacturer's energy manufacturing choice, it is depend on which the country's people prefer to use which kinds of energy for their daily life needs.

However, scientists predict secondary energy market will have large market share, due to primary energy will have shortage to explore to supply in our earth and future energy consumers(users) prefer to choose to use more efficiency, less energy consumption, none environment pollution cause, cost effectiveness, renew to use of any kinds of energy. For example, the electricity recharge battery secondary man-made renew used energy is one kind of reducing air pollution power to push any electric battery vehicles to be driven to compare gas energy during drivers are driving their cars on the roads. They can reduce noise and air pollution and drivers can drive safely, who only need to buy one electric recharge battery to recharge in any electric recharge battery stations on streets when the electric recharge battery has no enough power to push their cars and they need to recharge their electric recharge battery drive when they had driven between one to two days. Due to primary energy, e.g. fuel , gas, the kinds of primary energies will have shortage to supply to global drivers to drive their traditional cars. Thus, the electric recharge battery or any undiscovered secondary energy will be future driving market needs. So, man-made renew used secondary energy, e.g. biofuel, hydro-electric, nuclear, will be one kind of efficient, clean, less pollution cause, cost-effective of energy to supply to our global vehicle market, even any other undiscovered new markets. Supposing they are popular to be used for electric vehicle market globally in future one day, then their prices will be decreased and constructed to average car requires up to 1,700 gallons of oil. Also supposing that making average computer requires more than ten times or weight to fossil fuels, every calories of food eaten in the US requires roughly then calories of fossil fuels. Hence, cheap energy will be one successful factor to influence future potential energy consumer (user) individual choice needs. Conversely, ion good economic times, people are more willing to travel, to buy products, and all of which success demand and low process for energy.

In the future, secondary energy will be the best choice to food production market. The modern food production system is essentially a success of changing fossil fuels into food. So, raising energy prices are almost higher food costs and even shortage for fossil fuels energy. If one day, one kind of discovered secondary man-made renew used energy can supply to any restaurants or homes to be used to cook at the cheap price, then the profit is very high for this kind of food production energy. Thus, future food production secondary energy consumption market is large and because the primary energy inputs for agriculture are higher than the energy outputs of the food. However, future secondary man-made renew used energy for food production system is only one part of whole energy consumer in food industry. The food production is related to whole food consumption market which includes: household cooking energy market, agriculture or vegetable, rice, fruit etc. foods farming machines energy market, food manufacturing factories market, food machine package market, transportation food delivery market, supermarket or fruit/food sale stores market. They must need any energy inputs to achieve the food production or food transportation or warehouse / stores electricity supply or cooking energy needs. Hence, these food suppliers relate to any whole food factory manufacturers, food retailers, food wholesalers, farmers and home/restaurant cookers, all of them must need to use energy to carry on their food producing or food cooking or food transportation activities every day in overall food industry. Thus, it seems that undiscovered any second energy demand will be increased, when the primary energy supply number is decreasing. Also, when people can accept to use secondary energy to replace primary energy to be used for any cooking, transporting food, manufacturing food, food retail stores or warehouse food delivery energy need activities. Then, the secondary energy price will be fall down to attract many food energy consumers.

Nowadays, the food industry energy may includes primary nature resource gas energy or electricity energy for house house families or restaurants cooking needs, food delivering lorry drivers driving needs usually. If future second man made renew used energy is invented successful popular to be used, e.g. hydrogen, electric recharged battery energy for electric vehicles or restaurant/home families cooking needs or food factories machine maufacturing energy needs. Then, the seconday energy will have possible to replace primary energy to be food industry energy market.

Wiley, composition services graphics indicated that global primary energy consumption had been increasing 30 billion tons from 1830 year to 510 billion tons in 2010 year as well as global population size had been increasing from 70 billion 1830 yeat to 510 billion in 2010 year. Thus, it seems that global primary energy consumption will be needed largely after 2010 year. If future global nature resource primary energy is explored full number and it had not enough energy number to supply global human to use. Then, it will being many people feel uncomfortable and inconvenient,e.g. Some countries won't have enough energy to supply transportion tools to be driven, some homes and restaurants won't have enough energy to supply to cook to eat or to provide restaurant clients to eat etc. daily activies, due to human's much activities which are needs energy supply. Thus, it seems that global primary energy comsumption will be needed largely after 2010 year.

Wiley, composition services graphics also explianed that why the primary energy consumption demand can be needed to achieve the same level to the global population size increasing in 2010 year. The graph showed these reasons why cause the same level of global population size and global primary energy consumpion demand which may include: The graph showed that after a nation is developed, its per-person energy use hegins to level off. In North Ameruca and Europe, where energy demand has remaincd flat, or fallen dightly, in each of the past few years. But the 1.3 billion people on those two continents are far outweighted by the 5 billion people in Asia and Africa, e.g. Chinese and Indian. who currently have more energy need to comapre average per man to North America and Europe per man, ensuring that overall energy demand will rise for years to come.

Wiley, composition services graphics also predicted that the growth in primary energy demand. China will have 4,500 million tons in 2035 year. India will have 3,000 million tons in 2035 year. Other developing Asia will have 2,000 million tons in 2035 year. Russia will have 1,500 million tons in 2035, Middle East will have 1,300 million tons in 2035, other rest of world will have 1,000 million tons in 2035. Hence, it implied that China will be the largest primary energy need country in the future.

China will be future the primary potential energy consumer market. The primary energy includes water, coal, wind, fossil oil, gas ,solar, geothermal energy, biomass (organiz material) etc. different natural resource primary energy. Otherwise, US, UK, Europe will be secondary energy potential need market. For example, electrical recharge battery energy will be raised demand to supply to any future new design electrical charge battery vehicles in US, Europe, UK markets.

Due to US, Europe, UK people concern environment protection, so they will invent many electric charge battery vehicles to consume electrical charge battery to replace polluted gas energy to avoid air pollution when the drivers are driving cars on themselve countries' roads. For example, second man-made renew used nuclear energy can be applied to rockets to pusch them to leave our earth to fly to other space far away and consuming nuclear energy will be cost efficient, and nuclear energy saving will be more when nuclear to spend long time to be used in any long time space journey. Hence, nuclear energy and electric charge battery secondary energy will be popular to be applied to vehicles and rockets energy needs in US, Europe, potential marketss, even our daily energy needs in global second energy market.

Who are your energy business's competitors (peers)? How do they compare? How have your energy business company performed cyclically? How to choose to manufacture to sell which kinds of primary or secondary energy product(s), either manufactures only primary energy product(s) or manufactures only secondary energy products or both? Which countries do you plan to sell your energy product?

Illustration by Wilsey, composition services graphiss showed that these natural resources to energy product the world's electricity percentage, such as below:

41% of coal, 5% of oil, 21% of gas, 13% of nuclear, 16% of Hydro, 3% other renewable secondary man-made energy. Hence, coal will be future the major natural resource to produce electricity. The energy entrepreneur ought attempt to explore any coal resources, when who choose to supply electricity power to consumers for future energy consumption country markets.

Wiley, composition services also predicted that the expectation is that North America coal will supply the expectation is that North America coal will supply Asian demand, Us export terminals have a total capacity of 173 million tommes output. China will drive 16% of the nations total output. China will drive the sea-born demand for coal over for the forcessable future. Chinese energy consumption will grow more than 12 % between 1980 and 2009 years. Though, China heads global demand, India is growing faster in terms of coal imports. Much of the global coal demand will be supplied by Indonesia and Australia. Colombia, Russia, South Africa and Mongolia are also players in global export coal energy resources.

Hence, environment scientists' education messages influence Greece householders believe that secondary energy will be one kind of new energy product to replace traditional primary energy product for human energy consumption market global needs. Hence, it is right time any energy entrepreneur needs to research how to explore any undiscovered man-made renew used secondary energy products to avoid primary energy shortage crisis occurrence. Greece householders will be the highest population number to choose secondary energy to replace primary energy to use at homes. it means that environment scientists had changed Greece householders' energy consumption behaviors at homes.

In conclusion, different countries will have different factors influence how the country's householders energy consumption behavioral changes. Hence, it seems that any country's householders' energy use of consumption behaviors will be possible influenced by extermal environment factors influence. Also, every country's energy providers can attempt to find whether the country has what kinds of unique factors to influence its householders' energy consumption efficiency to increase or decrease in order to find the methods to solve the energy efficiency demand reducing challenges successfully.

CHAPTER NINETEEN

How artificial intelligence impacts energy consumers using behaviours

Nowadays, many countries began to educate citizens who have responsibilities to use energy at homes or offices or public places or any indoor environments in avoiding to do energy wastage behaviours or misuse energy wastge attitudes as well as teaching them have responsibilities to protect their earth's natural environment to reduce air, water pollution in order to void rising temperature to bring globl warm challenge to influence our quality of life to be poor, even facing death threat, due to our natural environment is damaged and polluted by our energy wastage behaviours.

In fact, I feel the energy wastage eduction is not one efficient or effective method to persuade every energy consumers, such as householders, office workers, factories workers, any entertainment places workers or enjoyers, such as cinema service staffs, shopping center staffs etc. entertainment places to reduce to use any electricity for light or any entertainment aims to consider themselves working environment or entertainment environment to satisfy, e.g. cinema movie to satisfy customers' needs. For example, private vehicle drivers, public transportation tool drivers, householder energy users, businessmen energy users who still only consider themselves passengers comfortable aims, e.g. spending much electricity often to turn on light in buses, taxi, cars, trams, trains, underground trains in morning or afternoon time. So, these public transportation tools are popular to waste electricity because they expect their passengers to feel comfortable in summer , so they will often turn on air conditioners to keep colder in summer or turn on warmers to keep warmer in winnter all the transportation working hours. So, these drivers are doing energy wastage behaviours. Moreover, these private car drivers only expect to feel comfortable , so they will open air conditioners to keep colder in summer when they are driving cars, even they are stopping cars on the road. So, they are also waste energy.

Hence, they will be negligent to consider how to use energy in efficient attitudes or energy saving behaviors in order to avoid energy shortage challenge occurrence. However, since (AI) technology began be popular to be accepted to use by human. (AI) scientists began to carry on researching how to apply (AI) technologies, e.g. big data gathering , robotics to assist human to adapt or learn to use any kinds of energy in efficient and no wastage attitudes or using behaviours habitually.

I shall explain how to apply (AI) technology to assist human to adapt to use energy in order to avoid to do energy wastage behaviours easily to every energy users as below:

In consumer psychological view point, the behaviours of individuals can have a standard rational choice model, in which people, such as energy users objectively weigh up the costs and benefits of investing time and money into " greening" their homes or offices or any working places or entertainment places or transportation tools being more energy efficiently. So, the social, cognitive and behavioural factors are important in explaining why many energy users, such as householders, vehicles owners or public transportation tool drivers, office workers, businessmen who are neglient to avoid to spend much excessive energy to drive their vehicles on the roads , to turn on lights in offices or any working environment or entertainment places or at homes all days. When they feel that they need more enjoyment, raising productivity, raising service performance to satisfy customers' needs. So, when they weigh economic benefits and cost. They will choose to use more energy to achieve their profit growth or customer number growth or improving quality of life intentions.

Hence, it also explain why education method is not effective to achieve energy saving aim for every energy users, e.g. it has no reward to compensate to their losses, when they choose to reduce energy consumption to cause that they have economic losses. So, it seems any country's government or schools energy saving education method which won't achieve the best energy saving consequency nowadays.

Why does (AI) influence energy users to reduce and use more energy in order to achieve their energy -saving habitual impact easily than education method? I shall explain as below:

(AI) technology can be one auto-manual tool to help householders to protect their homes to be more green environment and be more energy efficient. For example, householders can install (AI) auto-energy efficient measurement tool to record whether they will spend how much money for energy . e.g. electricity , gas consumption at home every day. So, they can know whether they will pay how much money for electricity or gas fee. (AI) auto-energy efficient measurement tool can also change householders' energy consumption behaviours to save more electricity or gas when they discover that the day' electricity or gas using number is excessive to cause they will be pay more extra electricity or gas expenditure on the day. Then, they will find whether why or how or what reasons cause them to spend excessive electricity or gas energy at homes, then they will change their energy wastage behaviours to save energy more easily. So, their energy -saving behaviours are influenced by the (AI) auto-energy efficient measurement tool's daily electricity or gas using record at homes.

So, (AI) auto energy efficient measurement tool can help householders to save energy and money when they need to use electricity or gas energy at homes. But making the kind of improvements that have these effects is not always simple, they usually require some planning, time to prepare to adapt how to do avoiding energy wastage behaviours at home habitually . So, (AI) auto-energy efficient measurement tools can focuse on what householders might be able to do and further encourage the uptake of energy efficiently measures as well as it might be able to motivates householders to act through restructuring existing incentives and using collective rewards.

When, they discover that the (AI) auto energy efficient measurement tool shows either electricity energy or gas energy or both using energy number is excessive too much to compare the normal energy using number on the day suddenly. Then , they will attempt to find what reasons influence their energy spending number is excessive on the day, in order to change their energy using behaviours or habits and they will be more acceptable to adapt to do energy saving behaviours because they can earn energy expenditure saving rewrd and money saving reward in order to avoid further the excessive energy using number to be increased to pay more electricity or gas energy expenditure , due to they often do unnecessary energy using habitual behaviours at homes.

Hence, (AI) auto-efficient energy measurement tool will have much effort to persuade householders to choose to do energy saving behaviours habitually at homes, due to it can provide the more acceptable number concerns their daily electricity and gas energy using record at homes to let them to know how and why their energy expenditure changes to spend more suddenly in order to let they can understand the reasons why and how cause their needs to pay extra excessive energy expenditure at homes.

The main important reward is that the householders can be encouraged to measure their energy using number and find the reasons why and how their energy using behaviours cause their extra excessive energy using number on the day. Then, they can find what the factors are to cause their electricity or gas energy using number to be increased suddenly on the day and change their energy using behviours to avoid the energy using number to be continus increased in order to avoid to pay extra excessive electricity or gas fees on the month immediately.

6.1 How to apply (AI) technology to improve energy efficiency and better climate change and the security of energy supply as well a resource efficiency?

Increasing energy efficiency involves using a reduced quantity of energy to achieve the same or improved product, process or sevice. It is generally measured in a physical unit as the ratio between energy output and energy input. Similarly, resource efficiency refers to the ability to use a reduced quantity or volume of resources to produce the same or an improved service or product and it is measured as the ratio betweenn useful material output and material input, both measured in physical terms (Dahlstrom and Ekins, 2005).

Hence, if it was only (AI) technology can increase energy efficiency or reduce resource effifiency to improve service performance. Then, it will reduce energy wastage. So, it bring this question: How to apply (AI) tool to reduce resource consumptin indentified by analysis of historical resource efficiency?

It presents an historial analysis that seems have relationship between energy and resource efficiency improvements and resource consumption across a number of different sectors of activity, including iron, and steel production, electricity generation from coal, oil and natural gas and motor vehicle travel.

So, future(AI) technology needs to fight social and behavioural barriers to energy efficiency in the housing sector. If future (AI) technology can improve energy efficiency for home renovations and it can consider the social factors. It is a qualitative investigation technology of the decision making process guiding to teach householders hoe to use overall energy was reduced by the householders' house renovation. It will also bring another question: How can (AI) technology can help householders to do decision making to reduce overall energy consumption by householders' houses renovation, such as reducing energy using when the householder needs to renovate whose house's design, e.g. extensions and additional bedrooms or bathrooms . So, future (AI) technology can be needed to help low income householders to increae energy efficiency and reduce energy consumption when their homes need to renovate whose houses' design ,e.g. extensions and additinal bedrooms or bathrooms or bookrooms or children toy rooms at hoomes.

Due to low income householders were concerned about energy consumption for environment and economic reasons, upfront costs rather than life-cycle costs were considered more important when the low income householders need to renovate to extend extra bedrooms, bathrooms, studyrooms to buy extra electronic appliances to install them in these rooms to use. Then, they will be concerned energy awareness how will be more consume when the low income householders choose to renovate their homes design to extend more rooms to feel more comfortable, or large size, but they also need to consume or use more electrciity or gas energy for extra electronic appliances in these rooms possible as the same time.

Hence, future (AI) technology needs to assist these low income householders how to reduce or avoid to ue extra more energy, when they renovate their homes' designs to cause to need to buy extra more electric appliances to use more electricity or gas energy at homes. Moreover, future (AI) technology ought have effort to help any countries' buildings to be efficient energy saving buildings to be efficient energy saving buildings to help householders to use less energy to live in their builsing efficiently. When the country's overall buildings can use energy efficiently , it won't only bring energy saving benefits, even it can bring the country's economic cost to be reduced , due to any building' energy efficient using high technological method. So, future (AI) energy saving technology will concentrate on how to help any buildings to use energy efficiently , in order to achieve energy -saving efficient buildings to let the householders and office energy users to either live or work in energy -saving efficient buildings to avoid energy wastage aim.

Hence, future (AI) energy -saving technology needs to focus on how changing energy users' energy wastage behaviours to energy -saving behaviours. How to apply (AI) energy-saving technology to assist energy users change their behaviours to spend unnecessary excessive energy to use habitually daily.

I recommend that future (AI) robotic cans be such as energy-saving machines to help any factory workers to cooperate to work to achieve efficient energy -saving aim, but they can also raise productivities. So, factory robotic are as learning tools, allowing factory energy users (factory workers) to teach themselves how to use less energy to achieve the productivity won't be decreased intention. So, when the robotics and factory workers work in the factory environment together. The robotics can give feedback to let these factory workers how to cooperate to use lesser energy to work efficiently in factories.

Other information and advice achieving better understanding and control of energy use in factory. So, future factory robotic machine men are such as teachers teach students in classrooms or trainers provide training to train trainee in factories. It means that robotics and factory workers can learn how to understand to do every working steps to avoid to spend extra excessive energy , but they can also raise productivities as the same time in factories.

So , future (AI) robotics will be demanded to invent to be one energy-saving machines to assist factory workers to use lesser energy to manufacture any products in manufacturing process, but they can also have productivity and efficiencies won't be reduced in the efficient team work method. So, every factory robotic machine mman is needed to be designed to own the advanced manufacturing technological skills or manufacturing methods to assist the factory workers to manufacture the kind of products in team work together in order to shorten time and using the most efficient manufacturing methods to achieve and produce the best quality products and the highest productivity in energy-saving working environment in factories. For example, when every team watch factory's factory workers who need to operte with ten workers per team in the watch manufacturing factory. One robotic machine with ten workers per team will need to raise to manufacture at least fifty watchs number per hour to compare only ten workers per team can manufacture the maximum fifty watchs number per house, when the robotic machine participates to every team to work together.

The robotic machine must need to help them to use lesser time and electricity energy to manufacture more than fifty watches number pe hour in order to achieve long tem energy saving and time saving and efficient raising productive economic benefits to the watch manufacturing company. Hence, the watch factory's every watching manufacturing robotic machines can encourage the watch manufacturing firm to choose to use them to assist every team watch manufacturing workers to work in order to achieve high efficient productivities, high quality of watch manufacturing, reducing every watch manufacturing , reducing every watch manufacturing time and the important intention is energy -sving efficient benefit to reduce to spend more extra excessive electricity for long term expenditure.

So, in the future , every robotic machine will need have these benefits to satisfy manufacturers' every -saving needs in their participative manufacturing process in order to achieve energy expenditure to reduce for long term economic benefits to persuade them to use these energy-saving efficient robotics in factory attractively.

Chapter Twenty

The relationship between consumer psychology and behavior

Can every consumer himself/herself personal psychology influence whose consumption behavior how to do final purchase decision? Why and how can psychological factor influence consumer behavioral change? Must psychological factor be the major influence to cause any consumers to make final purchase decision? Can other factors influence psychological factor to influence consumers final purchase decision?

I shall indicate online shopping method, how online shopping consumers are influences to make final purchase choice from their psychological changing influence. In fact, it may have different factors to influence consumer behavior towards online shopping. Usually online buyers will choose to buy any things, when they stay at home in preference. They feel turn on home computer to shopping in preference, due to They feel turn on home computer to apply internet channel to buy any things will be more safe to compare to use public libraries, shopping centers, schools, office computers' internet to buy any things. It is one good example to explain why online shoppers usually like to buy any things to turn on home computer internet to spend much time to choose to buy any things. Safety feeling psychological factor is one important factor to influence online shoppers prefer to turn on home computer to apply internet channel to buy any things . It is possible that they feel public places' computers are Insafe and their visa cards personal data will be theft by any one easily.

Due to online shopping method has risk to bring any online shoppers' visa card personal data loss or theft. So, safety psychological factor will influence many online shoppers choose to apply internet transaction tool to buy any things at home. Unless, the online shopper has no computer at home or whose computer has no internet installation to his/her computer. Then, he/she only chooses to use public computer internet to buy any things. Hence, it explains that safety psychological factor can dominate or control any online shoppers' purchase behaviors to choose where is the most suitable place to use computer internet to carry on online shopping buying action. Also, it explains safety or privacy factor (avoiding visa card data theft) which will be one important factor to influence online consumers' preference purchase place choice (turning on the place's computer and applying its internet to carry on online shopping actions). Even, time factor and convenient both factors will not influence general online shoppers' using home computer and internet tool purchase behavior. For example, one student is staying at whose school library place at this moment, his school library's computer has installed internet too, he plans to buy one book for his reference at this moment. Although, he can apply this school library's computer internet to buy this book immediately. But, when he feels that he can buy this book immediately , if he decides to apply his school's library computer website to find any book shops , whether they have this book to sell to him. Possibly, he only needs to spend more ten minutes, or less than ten minutes to buy this book. SO, he does not need to spend longer time to catch any public transportation tools to go home and he also needs much time to turn on home computer to search any online book shops' websites to buy this book from himself home computer internet channel. However, it is due to privacy and safety psychological factor influence where is the most suitable place choice to buy this book from internet channel. SO, it explains that why psychological factor will be more important preference to compare time and convenient factors to influence online shoppers' (online shopping place) choice.

How psychological factor influences women /men (females/male) shopping place) choice. Shopper behavior has focuses on individuals and the factors that impact their decisions to spend their resources on consumption –related items. Female and male's consumption model or behavior has different, due to their sex is different. So, their psychology are also different to influence their shopping behaviors in possible. For example, women think differently from men because there are biological , neurological and behavioral variations between the brains of men and women . This differences in turn make an impact on their shopping behavior. When, men will load themselves with sufficient information of a product or service through internet, advertising, reviews. Otherwise, women would try to get benefit from others' shopping experience by asking peoples' ideas before they choose to buy any products.

Retail is the dominion of women and shopping is an action frequently seen as complementary to female role. IN general, female like to go to supermarkets, or any food shops to buy any kinds of food more than male. Women go on shopping to purchase both essential and discretionary products (daily living useful products), more than male. Females (women) are considered to be the most potential household consumers, as it has almost 80 percent of the domestic expenditure is spent by female to every householder (family member shoppers).

Any family member mother or sister will be the influential role. Female is the influential member , she can make final purchase decision in any householder (family) usually. It is possible due to any family member father or son has more confidence to believe mother or sister whose final purchase decisions are more accurate judgement before they pay to buy any things for home to use or eat. Hence, this female's accurate shopping judgement influence role or feeling which is one major psychological factor to explain that why householder female member can be the final shopping decision maker more than male member in any householder, because they are felt to be one confident home shopper to every male family member. In general, they are felt to make more reasonable or accurate judgement to buy any kinds of products or food for home to use or eat to compare male family members' shopping judgement. Nowadays, it also explains why " confidence" is one important psychological factor to influence female, which is the major influential final shopping decision making more than male at any homes.

How can psychological factor influence either online or offline (visiting shops) shopping behavioral choice? Traditional shopping (visiting shops) had been one kind habitual consumption model or method, but internet shopping method had been also popular to be accepted to young people, e.g. student shoppers, even old people who also accepted to use internet to shopping. However, psychological factor is one important factor to influence their shopping method changing.

Online shopping is real fact in recent years. It will bring innovative and high technological shopping method to change traditional visiting shops shopping method as soon future. IN nowadays shopping environment, consumers like to buy any things conveniently in short time. Busy working and living factor influence their shopping feeling to be changed. IN general, consumers do not like to spend much time to visit any shops to choose any products and make final purchase decision. They like to make purchase decision in short time immediately. Due to internet is convenient, consumers they do no need to find where the shop can sell the product. They only need to turn on computer and enter any websites to search whether which online shop provides the kind of product to let them to bur from internet. Convenience and fun and high technological internet shopping method will be one kind of attractive shopping method to replace traditional visiting shops shopping method to change any one of consumers their traditional and habitual shopping model (method) or consumption behaviors daily.

The reason may be busy working time psychological factor to working people as well as busy learning time psychological factor to students. Convenient shopping factor, high technological invention of electronic shopping method factor. Many students and working people hope to spend less time to choose whether any product is the most suitable product to buy. They do not want to spend much time to search which shop can sell the product. Working and learning time is more important to compare shopping time. Hence time psychological factor will influence many young consumers choose to buy any things form internet channel. Otherwise, old people are retirement, they have much time to relax or entertain. SO, usually old people do not like to apply internet to buy any products at home. Because they have much time to visit any shops to go to shopping . Hence, psychological time factor will influence the shopping choice behavior difference between young age consumers and old age consumers.

Why can product knowledge psychological factor influence consumers product choice behavior? If the consumer feels the brand's any products have better to quality to compare other brands' products. He has confidence and product knowledge to use the brand's product. He has good past purchase experience to use the brand's products, because his useful feeling is good and he feels the brand's product can satisfy his need to use it. His past useful experience of this brand's product psychological factor will cause his future preference purchase choice , when he feels need to buy same or similar product in marketplace. So, it implies that when the consumer has good purchase and useful experience to the product, he will repeat to buy the brand's product again. Otherwise, when the consumer has bad purchase and useful experience to use the product before, he will lose confidence to buy the brand's product again. Hence, it explains why whether the consumer's good or bad purchase and useful experience psychological factor will influence whose purchase choice either repeat purchase or not repeat purchase again to the brand product.

Marketing message (unique value) and advertising campaigns influence psychological factor, it can influence consumers' confidence to use the brand's any products, even increase sales, because if the brand product seller can build good image to let consumers (public) to know its products existence by television, radio, newspapers, internet advertising channel. So, it seems that public advertisement promotion method can build good image to any product, it can achieve good image psychological factor to persuade any customers to attempt to buy the product to use or buy the food to eat. It is one building good image to let consumers to know the brand existence in the marketplace, it can bring message concerns that whether what kinds of products it is selling, how much price, discount it charges, what advantages of its products. All of these advertising message may persuade any customers to make first time purchase choice or repeat purchase decision, when they are watching its product advertisement from television, listening its advertisement from radio, reading its advertisement from newspapers or magazines etc. different advertisement channels in any time easily.

Any one of its advertisement message can let any audiences to remember the product's shape, color, size in their brains in long time. SO, long time advertisement memory to the product , it will bring positive consumption image influence to any audiences as well as persuading them to make final purchase choice to the product more easily.

Hence, advertising can shorten any consumers' purchase process or choice time to the product. Consumer behavior refers to the selection, purchase and consumption of products and services for the satisfaction of their wants. There are different processes involved in the consumer behavior. Initially the consumer tries to find what commodities, he would like to find what commodities, he would like to consume, then he selects only those commodities that promise greater utility. After selecting the commodities, the consumer makes an estimate of the available money which he spend. Lastly, the consumer analyzes the prevailing prices of commodities and takes the decision about the commodities he should consume usually. Hence, one attractive advertisement can influence many consumers feel that they do not need to spend much time to compare different kinds of similar products (product selection time), because the advertisement had attract their consideration to make final purchase decision. Hence, one attractive advertisement can shorten any consumers' (product selection time) to compare different kinds of products in order to make final purchase decision. Because it has build confidence to let many audiences feel the brand's products are worth to buy to compare other brand's products.

On conclusion, above these consumer behavioral purchase cases explain why consumer individual psychological factor can influence his/her final purchase decision. It implies that it has close relationship between consumer psychology and behavior. How the consumer's feeling to the product, it will cause his purchase behavior either selecting purchase it or selecting another product to replace it effect. SO, psychological factor is one absolute important factor to influence consumer behavior.